What Happens When Women Walk in Faith

LYSA TERKEURST

HARVEST HOUSE PUBLISHERS
EUGENE, OREGON

Cover by Connie Gabbert Design + Illustration

Cover photo © Rawpixel.com / Shutterstock

Backcover author photo by Amy Riley Photography

What Happens When Women Walk in Faith
Copyright © 2005 by Lysa TerKeurst
Published by Harvest House Publishers
Eugene, Oregon 97408
www.harvesthousepublishers.com

ISBN: 978-0-7369-7264-2 (pbk.)
ISBN: 978-0-7369-7265-9 (eBook)

The Library of Congress has catalogued the earlier printing as follows:
TerKeurst, Lysa.
    What happens when women walk in faith / Lysa TerKeurst.
        p. cm.
    ISBN-13: 978-0-7369-1571-7
    ISBN-10: 0-7369-1571-0
    1. Christian women—Religious life. I. Title.
    BV4527.T464 2005
    248.8'43—dc22   2005001912

Printed in the United States of America

20 21 22 23 24 25 / BP-CD / 13 12 11 10

To my two beautiful sons, Jackson and Mark.
Through you, God has made my feet walk paths
that I never knew could be so amazing.
From the first night you called me "Mom,"
my heart and life has never been the same.
I lovingly dedicate the words penned here to you.

Contents

Introduction 7

Phase One: Leaving
1. The Map 13
2. A Line in the Sand 21
3. God Has a Plan 29
4. Loving God More than My Dream 37

Phase Two: Famine
5. The Adventure Our Souls Were Made For 49
6. God's Extraordinary Invitation 57
7. God Is with You 67
8. Refusing to Get Bogged Down in Bitterness 75

Phase Three: Believing
9. A Most Unlikely Path 85
10. Roadblocks and Reassurances 93
11. God Will Make a Way 103
12. Learning to Lead 111

Phase Four: Death
13. Death Does Not Mean Defeat 125
14. Pressing Through the Pain 135
15. God Isn't Surprised by Death 143
16. God's Portion, Position, and Promise 151

Phase Five: Resurrection
17. God's Dream, God's Way 165
18. A Promise Made Is a Promise Kept 175
19. God Brings Dreams to Life 185
20. Every Promise Fulfilled 193

Notes 203

Introduction

I BELIEVE GOD GIVES EVERY WOMAN a dream. Not the *same* dream, of course, but a dream that is especially tailored for her talents and His purposes. Each woman receives a dream that only she is destined to fulfill.

But just as the Israelites were promised a land flowing with milk and honey only if they had the faith to move ahead and *take* the promised land, so too does every woman with a dream face obstacles that would keep her from God's best for her. The Israelites had to overcome giants in the land. Those giants struck fear in the heart of those to whom the promise was given. Some drew back as a result. Discouragement set in. Fatigue, impatience, unbelief…all of these were common to those men and women who spent 40 years in the desert because they simply couldn't walk in faith toward the destiny God had called them to.

I meet many women who *know* in their hearts that God has great things for them. But with every advancing step, they meet obstacles. Giants are in their promised land. And they experience those same feelings of discouragement, fatigue, and unbelief.

I know these feelings not only from the women I meet but because I've experienced every one of them myself. I *still* face obstacles as I pursue what God has called me to. But in the past several years, as I've been willing to move ahead in spite of the obstacles, God has given me my dream.

Let me ask you this: What is the dream God has given you? Maybe you can't quite put it into words except to say that you know that God wants to use you. But *how* that's to happen...you're not quite sure.

Not knowing exactly how God wants to use you is okay. When a woman begins to walk in faith toward God, He will give the dream. For me, the dream has resulted in public speaking, writing, and the birth of Proverbs 31 Ministries. Your dream—the way God wants to use you—will probably be totally different. But though the dreams we have may be different, I've discovered that the path is very similar for most women. And walking that path by faith is what *What Happens When Women Walk in Faith* is all about.

In the following chapters, I want to talk to you about the five phases I've identified in the Bible common to people who have stepped out with God in pursuit of their dream. Throughout this book we'll see how different biblical characters weathered those five phases, and we'll learn how to recognize these phases in our own faith walk. I'll also be sharing with you many of my own adventures as I've progressed through these stages time and time again. I hope that as you better understand these phases of faith, you'll avoid the discouragement and defeat so many of us have gotten bogged down in along the way. You'll be able to press through, walk confidently, and avoid doubting God.

The five phases of faith go hand in hand with five fundamental truths of God:

1. God has a plan for me.
2. God is with me.
3. God will make a way.
4. God isn't surprised by death.
5. God brings dreams to life.

Keeping these five vital truths in mind will sustain you as you pass through the five phases of faith. As you'll soon discover, Satan will oppose you as you begin to fulfill your dream. He will suggest some lies that are in direct opposition to the five truths above:

1. God couldn't care less about you.
2. God is too busy with the important people to be bothered by insignificant you.
3. God isn't to be trusted.
4. Death means defeat.
5. Dreams only happen by chance.

These are the lies that Satan will use to kill your dream. The better we understand the difference between truth and lies, the freer we are to walk with God through the phases of faith and not get sidetracked.

These are the five phases of faith you'll pass through to achieve your dream:

1. Leaving: In order to go to a new level of faith with God, you've got to leave the old behind.

2. Famine: In this new place, you'll realize your comfort zone is gone, and you'll learn to depend on God like never before.

3. Believing: You've always wanted to really believe God, but now your experience of Him becomes too real to deny.

4. Death: Coming to the end of your ability to make things happen seems like death to you. But to God, this is the only way to new life with Him.

5. Resurrection: In a way only He could, God makes your dream come true. Only then do you understand

that real joy isn't in the dream itself but rather in the richer faith you acquired along the way.

So get ready, my friend. Strap your most comfortable walking shoes on. You've got a basic understanding of where we're headed, and now it's time to go. At the end of each chapter you'll find a Personal Bible Study. You'll find it helpful to get a notebook to record your answers and thoughts along the way. Take time to read the Scriptures, think about the questions, and record your responses in your notebook. Are you excited? I am. Indeed, walking with God takes you to amazing places!

PHASE ONE

Leaving

One

The Map

I FELT SO INSIGNIFICANT. So small. I made my way up to the speaker in the front of the room. She was surrounded by women of all ages. Some just wanted to give her a tearful hug. Others held her book in their hands, looking for a note of encouragement and an autograph.

I just wanted to ask her *how?*

How do I take a broken life and allow God to use it for His glory? Is it possible that a girl rejected by her earthly father could actually be chosen and set apart for a divine calling? Could God really have a purpose for *my* life just as He had for hers?

I waited in line for my turn. Then, as I opened my mouth to speak, my throat tightened, my eyes filled with tears, and all I could squeak out was an emotional *"How?"* I wanted her to take me home with her and teach me. I wanted her to pack me in her suitcase and whisk me away from my meaningless life and into the life of one making a difference. I wanted her to share some quick and easy answer, three easy steps to the life you dream of, all for the low price of attending the seminar. But this speaker wasn't a magician, a slick salesman, or a woman looking for a new houseguest. She was a woman who had experienced deep hurts and bitter disappointments and who had chosen to surrender her life—with all its failure and pain—to God. Now she was being used by Him in a truly wonderful way.

She did not give me the quick and easy answer I was looking for. She didn't give me any profound wisdom or direction. We only had time for her to simply tell me how she got started, and then I found myself making my way back to my seat. But I wasn't heading back empty and without hope. What this speaker lacked in words, she more than made up for in example. I had seen Jesus in her. I had seen living proof of God's redemption. I thought to myself, *If God could do that with her, I think there's hope for me after all.* And something new and big and God-directed was born in me and confirmed in my heart in an undeniable way that day.

God Will Fill in the Gaps

Though I still didn't know *how* God could possibly use me, I knew He could find a way. Though I didn't know *when* God could use me, I knew the timing was in His hands. Though I didn't even think I had much to offer, I knew God would fill in my many gaps. I simply knew God was calling me, inviting me, wooing me to something with His fingerprints all over it. And that was enough.

My life certainly didn't change overnight. I experienced a waiting period, a time of growth, development, and perseverance as God prepared me. Lessons on patience, trust, surrender, and learning to take hold all preceded my stepping out. But even in this seemingly unimportant time of pruning and trials, God was preparing me for the next step. This "getting ready period" was not a waste of time. It was an important part of fulfilling my calling. Though I couldn't see much fruit, God was getting my branches ready and healthy enough to hold all He knew was coming.

So I left the conference that day excited, only to be hit with a shocking dose of reality back home. There were still dishes to be washed, clothes to be folded, bottoms to be wiped, and everyday life to be dealt with. To be completely honest, I didn't like my mundane life. And yet what we call mundane is, in some very important ways, significant in God's school of preparation.

Dreams and Despair

I can remember as a young girl looking out my bedroom window, dreaming of the man I'd one day marry and the children I'd one day hear call me Mommy. I counted the years on my small hand and delighted as each one ticked away. With each passing birthday, my anticipation grew. Like most other girls, I had other goals and dreams, but the fairy tale of my heart was being a wife and mother. I could hardly wait!

Then all of a sudden I was an adult woman, and God had indeed blessed me with both a loving husband and wonderful children...and I was miserable.

How could this be? What kind of terrible joke was this, that the very thing I dreamed would bring me ultimate happiness had actually ushered me into a deep despair? How ungrateful I felt. I had asked, begged, pleaded for God to give me these gifts, and now I was desperately looking for the return policy.

Was I missing something genetically? As I looked around at church and the mall and the grocery store, I saw other women who seemed delighted to be the June Cleaver of my generation. They'd walk by me, giggling and cooing at their baby as if they were in a romantic movie. They mentioned offhandedly that their husbands were whisking them off to New York that weekend. These women were, of course, all skinny, and their well-ordered shopping lists gave evidence that their homes were no doubt tidier than mine.

What was wrong with me? I felt like a failure as a woman. And most disturbing was the fact that I didn't like being a mother. I was a gold-star member of the Mommy Guilt Club almost from the moment my child exited the womb. Can you imagine feeling this way and then considering that God was calling *you* into ministry?

Who do you think you are? Do you really think God could use a woman like you to help others? Satan's whispers were relentless. Sadly, to be honest, I agreed with him. At the conference, I had felt such assurance of God's calling, but back in the midst of everyday life, I began to doubt.

My only recourse was prayer. I got down on my knees and cried out to the Lord for His assurance. And as He always does, God met me there at the point of my need. He assured me that He doesn't call the qualified, but He qualifies those He calls.

Surrendering Inadequacy

My friend, I don't know where you are as you read these words. I don't know the circumstances of your life. I don't know the dream God has given you. Perhaps you don't either...yet. But I do know you have this book in your hands for a reason. God has a plan for you. A dream perhaps you can't even imagine, an assignment you can't figure out and wouldn't even dare to consider as being for *you*. I pray that as I have honestly shared the misgivings I had, you will find great hope that God really can use any woman who surrenders her inadequacies and circumstances to Him. I've seen Him do it time and time again in the lives of women who were willing to walk in faith. But most powerfully I've seen it in my own life.

Though it started small and happened slowly, I'm now able to live the dream God has given me. But also, and more importantly, I'm now a very happily married mother of five kids. I wake up most days excited about my life and can't wait to unwrap the blessings of serving, loving, and enjoying those whom God has entrusted to me.

Now don't get me wrong, I still have days when I feel like a failure, but they are fewer and far between. My circumstances haven't really changed since those early mommy days (except I have a lot more kids!), but my perspective certainly has.

Perspective is the key. If I'd never had the husband and the kids that I have, I'm convinced I would be incredibly self-centered and seriously lacking in character. God uses different things in different lives to shape and mold them, and my family was God's perfect tool for building my life. God used many everyday life experiences to shape and mold me for ministry. I learned so much by being faithful in little, everyday responsibilities, and eventually God was able to entrust larger responsibilities to me. Any woman who wishes to be used by God must be willing to honor God no matter what.

Honoring God

During those early years, God was asking me, "Lysa, as you start to feel overwhelmed with doing the laundry and caring for the kids and cooking meals and handling life, *will you honor Me?* Will you do it with a grateful heart? Will you see the blessings hidden in the long to-do lists? Will you surrender your plans of convenience and ease and accept My plans for your growth and maturity?"

When I aligned my perspectives with God's and I decided to honor Him in all things, big and small, I was finally ready to step out in ministry. My circumstances were not perfect, but I knew whose face to seek when I fell flat on my own. So I declared in my heart I was a woman in ministry, dedicated to serving God, and I started to watch for His invitation to join Him.

Trust me—those first steps were the furthest thing from limelight ministry. They were everyday choices to honor God right where I was: spending time in God's Word even when the items on my to-do list seemed more urgent. Getting filled with Him first so I could love and give and serve out of an overflow rather than relying on my own strength.

Honoring my husband even when he'd said something that hurt my feelings. Choosing to keep a good attitude even when the grocery store clerk overcharged me and took longer than necessary to remedy the problem. Having patience with my children and handling a problem calmly when I really wanted to yell and send them to their room. Graciously serving other people without calling attention to my service. Honoring Him in these ways was a vital part of getting my heart ready to serve Him in larger ways.

God wants us to honor Him. He wants us to put personal conveniences aside, lay our own ideas down, and get past our stubborn will to have and do things our way and in our time. God wants our obedience, not just lip service. It's one thing to say we'll honor Him but another thing entirely to actually do it. Don't wait for the perfect day to start honoring God. Make that choice today. Don't think you're not doing what God called you to do just because things don't seem as glamorous as you thought they would be. *If you are a woman who honors God right where you are, you are in ministry.* Keep being obedient, keep looking for the next open door of opportunity, and above all else hold closely to our Lord.

Personal Bible Study

1. Read Job 1:6; Luke 22:31; 1 Peter 5:8.

These verses show us how active Satan is in our world. His very name means "one who separates." His chief purpose is to separate us from God however he can. He wants us to chase after other things—even good things—so we miss God's best. He wants to keep us busy. He wants to fill our heads full of lies so that we can't hear God's truth. Too many times I have allowed his tricks to steer me down the wrong path. What about you? What tactics is he using to try to defeat you right now?

2. Read Ephesians 6:11; James 4:7; John 10:10.

Satan uses the same old bag of tricks, but we have God—who is infinitely creative—on our side. We can turn to Him as our support, wisdom, and way out under temptation (1 Corinthians 10:13). God gives us the strength to stand and the armor to protect ourselves from our enemy. Satan comes to steal our joy, to kill our spirit, and to destroy our hope. He masquerades as the angel of light, deceiving us with his false beauty (2 Corinthians 11:14). We must be aware of how he works so we can guard our minds, hearts, and steps as we set out on our amazing journey. Make no mistake, this is one trip Satan does not want you to take, and he will pull out every trick in his bag to try to stop you. Just remember the scriptural paradigm: Resist the devil and he will flee from you (James 4:7). Draw close to God and He will draw close to you (James 4:8).

In your notebook, list some practical ways to resist Satan.

List some practical ways to draw close to God.

3. Read Hebrews 10:35-36.

As we set out on our journey together, I want you to really ponder these verses. Copy them down in your notebook. This book is written to enable you to journey with confidence wherever God is leading in your life. Your journey will not look the same as mine—it is as unique as you are. But the same basic truths described in these verses apply to us all. Circle these words after you have copied down the verses: *confidence, perseverance,* and *promised.* My prayer is that you will find the confidence you need to persevere until you have received whatever God has promised you. Press on, my friend, and prepare to be amazed at what God has to show you through this study!

Hebrews 10:35-36

35. Do not, therefore, fling away your [fearless] confidence, for it has a glorious and great reward.

36. For you have need of patient endurance [to bear up under difficult circumstances without compromising], so that when you have carried out the will of god, you may receive and enjoy to the full what is promised.

Two

A Line in the Sand

TO HONOR GOD COMPLETELY, you need enough faith to leave with Him. *Leave?* Leave and go where, you ask? Leave the way you've always done life and start doing things differently with God. Leave the attitude, leave the stubborn pride, leave the right to be right, leave the control, and biggest of all, leave the unbelief.

Now wait a minute, you say. *I thought God was about to ask me to step up and do big things for Him, but you're saying the first step is leaving stuff behind?*

Absolutely.

A couple of years ago, I drove an old minivan. It got me where I wanted to go but lacked many of the comforts and conveniences a newer model would have given me. For one thing, the rearview mirror had fallen off the windshield. I went to get a repair kit, thinking I would repair it on my own and save a little money. But as I read the instructions to use the super-duper repair glue, fear seized my heart, and visions of disaster started dancing through my mind. The instructions were very bold with the warning that you must not let the glue get on your skin or you could literally get stuck to whatever you were gluing.

I am not a woman of great coordination, and most embarrassing things often happen to me. So I became convinced that I would be the one out of a million who would actually have to drive herself to the emergency room because her thumb was permanently stuck to the windshield! Instead, I tossed the kit and drove around with the rearview mirror in my cup holder and used it only when absolutely necessary.

Fortunately, I learned to use other means of navigating the road, such as using my side mirrors or asking other passengers in the car to check the traffic. What I soon learned was that using the rearview mirror wasn't nearly as necessary as I once thought it was. To be honest, I used it for the wrong reasons anyhow. I used it to put my makeup on while driving—dangerous and unnecessary. I used it to fuss at my kids while driving—dangerous and unnecessary. I used it to speed into the other lane when the driver in front of me was going too slow in my rushed opinion—dangerous and unnecessary. You see, looking behind you and ahead of you at the same time is impossible. Can you imagine how dangerous the roads would be if everyone drove around looking in their rearview mirrors only?

It's much safer to stay focused on the road ahead and use the rearview mirror when absolutely necessary.

Don't Look Back

This might be a silly example, but it makes a strong spiritual point. We can't go ahead with God to new and exciting places if we're spending too much time looking back. We must leave our past behind, draw a line in the sand, and determine to proceed *forward* with God. As a matter of fact, every time God calls His servants to go to new heights with Him, they have to go through a leaving process first.

In Genesis 7, we find Noah and his family being called by God to leave and go into the ark. Because of their obedience, their lives were spared, as was the entire race of mankind. In the book of Ruth, we find the widow Ruth making the tough decision to remain loyal to her mother-in-law, leave Moab, and travel to Bethlehem. Because of her obedience, she eventually finds a new husband, and through their lineage, Jesus is born. In 1 Samuel 16, we find Samuel being sent to anoint one of Jesse's sons to be the new king. David, the youngest and least likely candidate, was the one chosen. Almost immediately after being anointed king, he had to leave the fields and flocks to go to the palace. Another interesting thing to note is that he didn't go to the palace to sit on the throne right away. He had to first serve the existing king as a harp player. Because of his obedience in leaving, we get to read about one whom God called a man after His own heart.

Jeremiah 1 tells the amazing story of Jeremiah being called. "The word of the LORD came to me, saying, 'Before I formed you in the womb I knew you, before you were born I set you apart; I appointed you as a prophet to the nations'." To which Jeremiah replied, "I do not know how to speak; I am only a child" (Jeremiah 1:4-6).

Now listen to the Lord's response to Jeremiah, "Do not say, 'I am only a child.' You must *go* to everyone I send you to and say whatever I command you. Do not be afraid of them, for I am with you and will rescue you" (Jeremiah 1:7-8). Did you see the word "go"? Yes, indeed, Jeremiah left his old way of relying on his own ability and accepted a new way of thinking. Because he was obedient to trust God, God promised to give him every word and power to accomplish the mission before him. "Then the LORD reached out his hand and touched my mouth and said to me, 'Now I have put my words in your mouth. See, today I appoint you over nations and kingdoms to uproot and tear down, to destroy and overthrow, to build and to plant'" (Jeremiah 1:9-10).

In the New Testament, when Jesus called His disciples, the first thing they had to do was leave wherever they were and whatever they were doing to follow Him. "As Jesus was walking beside the Sea of Galilee, he saw two brothers, Simon called Peter and his brother Andrew. They were casting a net into the lake, for they were fishermen.

Come follow me, Jesus said, *and I will make you fishers of men.* At once they left their nets and followed him" (Matthew 4:18-20). Because of their obedience, we have a record of the life-changing actions and truths of Jesus.

Even when marriage is mentioned in both Genesis and Matthew, the mandate to leave is first. "For this reason a man will *leave* his father and mother and the two shall become one flesh" (Genesis 2:24; Matthew 19:5).

So is it any surprise that you will be called to leave as well? You may or may not have to change physical locations, but you will have to change your mind-set and your spiritual perspectives. Time and time again the formula for *starting something new* begins with *leaving the old.* Leaving is usually an act of obedience and not a desire of the heart. It is hard. It causes you to step outside of your comfort zone and enter a life that requires faith.

A Powerful First Step

I was teaching this principle at a weekend retreat once when a lady came up to me afterward and thanked me for the invitation to draw a line in the sand and leave her past behind. I had issued them a challenge: "Just because you came to this retreat one way doesn't mean you have to leave the same. If you came as a discouraged woman, leave *encouraged.* If you came defeated, leave *victorious.* If you came as a mom who yells at her kids, leave challenged *to make better choices.* If you came as a wife who doesn't honor your husband like you should, leave *renewed with new perspectives.* Wherever you fall short, let God fill in your gaps this weekend and empower you to leave changed. Experiencing life change is not a matter of chance, it's a matter of *choice,* choosing God's ways instead of your own."

With tears in her eyes, this dear woman hugged me and thanked me for giving her hope that things could be different—and permission to make it happen. A few months later, I received an e-mail from her telling me that she literally went home and drew a line on the ground. She lived in New Hampshire, so instead of drawing a line in the sand, the minute she drove in her driveway, she grabbed a hockey stick and drew a line in the snow. She stood behind her line and paused. She didn't want to make this declaration alone, so she beeped her car horn until her husband and all her children came out to greet her. She instructed them to come and stand behind the line with her.

Choking back tears, she told them she knew she had not been the woman of God she wanted to be or the wife and mom they deserved. But over the weekend, God had shown her some amazing truths, and she was making the choice to change. With that, her entire family held hands and stepped over the line together. Leaving is truly a powerful first step!

Was her life now going to be hunky-dory? No! Her circumstances were going to be just the same when she walked back through her threshold, but *she* was different. She was changing. She was determined to honor God and begin living a life that required faith. She would have to depend on God like never before.

Your New Name

What might you need to leave behind? How will you change as a result of leaving? What might the cost be? What will be your reward? Later in this section we'll be taking a walk with Abraham, who went through all five phases to fulfill the calling on his life. We'll pay special attention to the leaving phase. Abraham was obedient to leave, and in the middle of Abraham's journey something significant happens. I want to point this out while you are asking these tough "leaving" questions.

> When Abram was ninety-nine years old, the LORD appeared to him and said, "I am God Almighty, walk before me and be blameless. I will confirm my covenant

between me and you and will greatly increase your numbers." Abram fell facedown, and God said to him, "As for me, this is my covenant with you: you will be the father of many nations. No longer will you be called Abram; your name will be Abraham, for I have made you a father of many nations. I will make you very fruitful; I will make nations of you, and kings will come from you" (Genesis 17:1-6).

Now to paint the backdrop of what had been going on in Abraham's life, let's remember, he'd been disobedient to God. Thirteen years earlier he'd had a baby with his wife's maidservant. He was trying to make the dream God had planted in his heart come true through his own schemes and plans—through his own strength. Abraham had lost sight of God's ability to fulfill His promise. So God reestablished the promise, recast the vision, and breathed fresh life back into Abraham's dream. God told Abraham it was already done. Look at these words: "I have made you a father of many nations." Not I *will* make you a father of many nations, but *I have already done it.* In other words, God tells Abraham that He has everything under control.

And did you catch the previous sentence? God gives Abraham a new name. He was called Abram before this reestablished-covenant encounter, but every time afterward, he is referred to by his new name. *Abraham* means "father of many."

God renamed Abraham, and He has renamed you as well. When you go through the leaving phase, you are asked to leave much behind. But you don't walk from this place empty-handed. You are going equipped with a new name. I used to be Lysa—a broken, insecure, and unable woman. But when I chose to leave that behind and walk with God, I became Lysa—a holy, chosen, equipped-by-God woman with a dream! I am not looking back! Equipped with your map and now focused ahead, you are closer than you think to the faith you've always wanted.

Personal Bible Study

1. Read Hebrews 11.

We will refer to this chapter throughout this book, but I want you to take a moment now to read through it in its entirety. This chapter is known as "faith's hall of fame." As we begin this journey of faith together, the accounts in this chapter will inspire and encourage you. Record the names in Hebrews 11 in your notebook. What do you already know about them? Were they perfect people, or were they fraught with human frailties? Did they make all the right choices, or did their bad decisions become part of their learning process? Did God choose them because they were perfect saints, or were they ordinary people who trusted Him? Allow this chapter to minister to you as you reflect on the very imperfect people God has used in the past to do great things. He can use you too!

2. Read Isaiah 43:16-19; Philippians 3:12-14.

Walking in faith includes leaving the past behind. In the first chapter, we mentioned Satan's schemes to defeat us and separate us from God. One of his main tactics is to use our past mistakes to cripple us. He is so crafty at holding our past over our head, thus making us feel useless, ineffective, and unworthy. But God wants to do a new thing within you. He wants you to forge ahead, pressing on toward the promised land He has set before you, forgetting the failures of the past. While we all need to remember the Egypts God has delivered us from, we need to change our focus, throw away that old rearview mirror, and prayerfully seek His direction as we set out on our walk with Him.

After reading the verses in Isaiah, list some of your streams in the desert.

What does Philippians 3:12-14 say we're straining toward?

3. Read Psalm 147:4; Isaiah 62:2-3; Revelation 3:11-12.

Abraham, as we will see, eventually does have a son named Isaac. The name Isaac means "he laughs" because Abraham and Sarah both laughed when the Lord told them that they were going to have a son in their old age (Genesis 17:17; 18:12). Names do mean a lot to the Lord. He changed Abraham and Sarah's names. He told Abraham Isaac's name before he was even conceived. He also designated the name above all names for His only Son, Jesus. When we join God's family, He writes our names in the Book of Life. As He designates us as His beloved children, may we lay claim to our new names, which He has engraved in the palms of His hands (Isaiah 49:16). Do you know the meaning of your name? Do a little research today to find out what it means. Write the meaning of your name in your notebook and see if you can find a verse that correlates with the meaning of your name. Write down the verse as well and spend time thinking about how it applies to your life and God's plan for you.

Three

God Has a Plan

As I've pursued my dream, I've experienced the leaving phase and all the other phases of faith several times. But each time, God brings me to a stronger faith than I had before. That's God's plan, you know. His ultimate goal is to grow us to be more and more like His Son, who had incredible faith. I must always keep this in mind because, for some reason, God doesn't seem to want to do things my way or in a time frame that I would choose. So to leave some things behind, we need to learn that God has a plan and to *trust* His plan.

In so doing, we'll find that we must leave our old identity behind. We just learned in chapter two that God has given us a new name, but sometimes we try to put our new name on our old identity. I had to learn to leave my wrong perceptions of myself and my bitterness from my past. Strangely, I'd held onto these like a security blanket. I was used to operating in a private realm, keeping everyone at a safe distance. I always thought to be in ministry meant painting the façade that I was perfect. Only then would I be a qualified servant of God. I quickly learned that people aren't impressed with fake perfection—they're turned off and intimidated by it!

God wanted me to be honest and real. That was to be my identity. He wanted to shine His grace, mercy, love, and redemption through my faults, failures, and frailties. He wanted to make me strong with His strength. He wanted to be glorified in any and all good that would come from my ministry efforts.

As I've mentioned, my dream—the ministry God gave me—started very small, right within the walls of my home. Eventually, God led me to a lady who felt passionate about writing a newsletter to encourage women. I agreed to help her write and promote the small newsletter. The newsletter subscriptions grew, and other opportunities for ministry resulted. Our local Christian radio station invited us to come on the air to give short devotional thoughts. From there we started to receive invitations to speak at small groups.

So, with shaking knees, a quivering voice, and some of the saddest-looking outlines you've ever seen, I booked my first few small speaking engagements. Somehow, the ladies were touched and the ministry continued to grow.

A Bright Idea

Eventually, I got the bright idea to write a book. I typed out my outlines in chapter form, thought of some catchy chapter titles, slapped a cover sheet on the ragtag collection, and called it a book proposal. Another friend of mine, Sharon Jaynes, and I naïvely headed to the annual Christian Booksellers Association International Convention, fully expecting to find a publisher eager to publish our proposed books. After all, the hardest part of getting a book published was writing it, right? Well, I quickly learned that couldn't be further from the truth. The wave of rejection letters that littered my desk in the months that followed the conference dashed my great hopes and big dreams.

Had I heard God wrong? I really felt He'd told me I would write books that help women. So I'd tried to force the dream to come true with my own formula, and it failed miserably. In my own reasoning, I had planned the trip to the convention thinking if I needed to find a publisher, I'd better go where the publishers were. But my efforts produced nothing but disappointment.

God did have a plan for me. But His plan started much smaller than mine. He opened doors for me to write smaller articles for more newsletters and some magazines. But there were rewards for doing ministry God's way. I'll never forget the first time I saw my name as the author of a published article. God might as well have opened the doors to the library and told me to count the books if I could, for that's the number of books that would eventually come from Proverbs 31 Ministries. Not that I'd write them all but that women throughout the world would catch a vision for writing their messages and that I could have a part in giving them the courage to do so.

I believed that God would one day give me the chance to write a book, and I committed myself to wait on Him. I would no longer go chasing after publishers; I would wait until God brought one to me. I took my book proposals, placed them in a file, closed the drawer, and thanked God in advance for what would one day come to pass. *I believed.* I chose to embrace the leaving phase and trust God.

Reality Hits

Three years later, I wrote an article for a financial publication. To be completely honest, I thought it was one of the worst articles I'd ever written. But the article made its way into a publisher's hands who read it, loved it, and offered me a book contract. Only God could do such a thing! I think God wanted to make sure I knew that a book contract had a lot less to do with me and a lot more to do with Him working through me—in His timing.

I was doing the happy dance everywhere I went. God did it! God really did it! I don't think my feet hit the ground for days. I was going to be a published author. I was thrilled beyond belief until a stark reality hit me: Getting a book contract is one thing, but actually writing the book—all 50,000 words of it—is another thing entirely. Was I nuts? Why did I want this, could someone please remind me? Did I know 50,000 words? Did I even know 1000 words that I could somehow tangle together 50 different ways?

Though I was scared and unsure, I started gathering quotes and stories. I assumed a most authoritative writing voice and mechanically typed out my first 10,000 words. I sat back in sheer delight, realizing I would make my editor's first deadline. I was to send this first section of the book off to her for approval before continuing on. Like a proud mama of a newborn baby, I nervously let someone else hold my little darling. I couldn't wait to hear her glowing report of how beautiful and full of promise my words were. Instead, I got back two pages of corrections that could be summed up with two earth-shattering words: Start over!

I got down on my floor beside my computer, buried my face into the carpet, and wept out loud. Oh, how this rejection hurt! I had embraced the leaving phase and was excited to be moving on. This was a call to leave again. It shattered my perception of what God was doing. It reminded me once again that I must *leave* something behind in order to be able to move ahead.

My Plans and God's Plan

I realized I had two choices. I could cling to my dream and smother it to death, or I could release it and let my own attempts to do God's work fall to the ground. I chose the latter, even through my tears. With as much faith as I could muster, I placed my book in God's hands, and only then did I understand. God was calling me to simply lay my desire to write a book on the altar.

God did require a sacrifice, but it was not the entire book project. He let me use a substitute sacrifice. My substitute sacrifice was my first 10,000 words. The reward was a book where I found my place as my reader's friend rather than an official-sounding expert.

God's plan was perfect, and when I left *my* plans behind, God let me participate in *His*. Looking back, I wouldn't have wanted it any other way. I still remember holding that first published book in my hands. Seeing my name on the cover, leafing through the pages, and seeing God's fingerprints all over this project brought tears to my eyes. Once again, I was reminded that the book was not really about getting a book published. That was just an aside, a fringe benefit. The real treasure was walking with God through the project. Being reminded firsthand that God does indeed have a plan. Not just a good plan. Not even a really good plan. God has the perfect plan.

My new voice changed other aspects of my ministry as well. I tossed the crafty, sad outlines from the talks I'd been giving and traded them in for sharing the real me, the imperfect, desperate-for-God me. God honored my obedience and continued to unfold a plan that I could have never imagined.

Proverbs 31 Ministries has now grown into an international women's ministry with a team of dedicated women who have caught God's vision. The devotional thoughts have transformed into a daily radio program heard on more than a thousand stations. The little newsletter is now a 16-page, full-color monthly magazine. We have more than 20 speakers who carry the message of this ministry throughout the world. And what about that dream of vast words? The women associated with Proverbs 31 Ministries have published 21 books, and more are on the way.

Everyday People

I stand humbly amazed. My teammates stand humbly amazed. We are all average, everyday women. God certainly doesn't need us to do this ministry, but He allows us to be a part of it. God has a ministry assignment for you, and He wants you to join Him. Soon, you'll stand back in amazement as well.

At each of my speaking engagements, I set up a book table. Each title is a reminder to me. It may look like a little bundle of pages and words, wrapped in a cover, but to me it is so much more. The little seed of a dream to write books that would help others has sprouted and bloomed. These books take the messages God has given me and the other women on my team into places we could never go. They are His words on loan to us from Him. He uses these words to inspire, encourage, teach, and help other people. They are living proof that walking with God truly does take you to amazing places!

Are you ready to venture to your own unique and exciting places? Commit to leave your agenda behind, take God's hand, and hold on tight…the journey has just begun.

Personal Bible Study

1. Read Nehemiah 9:7-8; Acts 3:25; Galatians 3:6-9.

As we've already seen in Hebrews 11, God doesn't seek out perfect people to do His work. I mistakenly believed at first that I needed to be perfect to serve God effectively. I think many people believe the lie that they must achieve perfection in order to begin a life of faith. But I learned that God uses our imperfections and our willingness to share our mistakes to reach the hearts of the lost. As I speak to women all over the country, I share my mistakes, my clumsiness, and my most embarrassing moments. While I am sharing, I *watch*. I watch their laughter give way to relief. These women seem to be saying to themselves, *If God can use her, surely He can use me!* Are you waiting until you have arrived at perfection to step out in service to God? Are you afraid to show the real you for fear it will hinder your ministry? Don't be afraid to start where you are and be who you are. Blessed are the transparent, for they shall be used by God in a mighty way! How might God use you, weaknesses and all, to minister to other people?

2. Read John 10:9; Revelation 3:7-8.

When I stepped out in my own strength according to my own timing, God didn't seem to be opening any doors. I battled frustrations as I questioned my calling. I wanted everything to work out, and I wanted it to happen according to my timetable. I showed God my agenda and expected Him to oblige. What I missed was that He *is* the door. This was not about me checking off my to-do list of accomplishments, but about me drawing closer to Him. As that happened, He would open a door that no one could shut. The time in which I thought He was not moving was actually the time He was moving in my heart. As I kept His Word and proclaimed His name, He was preparing me to walk through the door. I would not trade that time for anything as I serve in ministry now. He used that time to equip me to fulfill my calling and to prepare me to reach women who needed to hear my story.

What do the sheep find when they walk through Jesus' door?

How does this encourage you?

3. Read Joshua 24:14-15; Psalm 68:6; 113:9.

In this chapter, I said that my ministry began right within the walls of my home. Never has this been more clear to me than as I reflect on God's plan for my life. He knew to give me exactly the parents, sisters, husband, and children He has given me to specifically prepare me for my calling. I know without a shadow of a doubt that I wouldn't be the person I am without these people as part of my foundation. They contributed to my character growth and played starring roles in my family dramas. I thank God for their influence in my life through the years, for better and for worse. *God has placed you exactly where you are according to His purposes.* Thank Him for that today. Write a commitment to not dwell on how some of these people have let you down. Thank God for using the people in your family to help shape and mold you for your calling.

Fixed mindset - the grasshopper
Mentality
vs
growth mindset

Four

Loving God More than My Dream

HOW ALIKE WE ARE TO THE CHILDREN OF ISRAEL. The Old Testament chronicles the history of the Hebrew people and the lessons they had to learn the hard way. They had to learn over and over and over again to leave some things behind.

Walking with God will indeed take you to amazing places—but it won't always be where you thought you wanted to go, and the road won't always be easy. To help prepare you for the things you'll learn, see, and experience on this journey, I want to explore rich biblical truths beginning with the stories of Abraham and continuing through the deliverance of the children of Israel.

As we start with Abraham and one of his first conversations with God, we shouldn't be surprised that God calls him to leave. Genesis 12:1-2 says, "The LORD said to Abram, '*Leave* your country, your people and your father's household and *go* to the land I will show you. I will make you a great nation and I will bless you; I will make your name great, and you will be a blessing.'" Verse 4 goes on to say, "So Abram left, as the LORD told him."

Amazingly, Abraham had to walk away from all that was comfortable—his family, his friends, and his wealthy lifestyle—in order to gain the blessings of the Lord. And I bet Abraham's understanding

Phase 1- Leaving

of becoming a great nation and being blessed was much smaller than God's amazing vision.

The same is true for our lives as well. Our thoughts about how God wants to use us are much too small. That is why we hesitate to leave our old ways behind. If we could taste the delights that await us in the promised land, we'd leave everything behind without hesitation…and yet God doesn't work that way. We must choose to leave *first*. We must see by faith the rewards ahead and then move toward them. What might God be calling you to leave? Check your answer with these other questions:

- Does it line up with Scripture?

- Would it cause me to become more like Christ in my thoughts and actions?

- Do I have a peace in my heart about this when I pray?

As you answer, I'd suggest you spend some time in prayer asking God to show you His answers, and then remember to look for confirmations from Him throughout your day and record them. These confirmations will prove invaluable as you move into the next phase that comes shortly after leaving—the phase I call famine…and the topic of the next four chapters.

Phase 2- Famine

A Famine in the Land

As we end our chapters on the leaving phase, I want to briefly alert you to the phases ahead so you see how they naturally unfold, one after the other, as God brings dreams to pass. Each new phase arises out of the previous phase and is an ongoing part of our life of faith. We will never arrive at a final stopping place in this life. We are always pilgrims here, looking forward to our final rest in heaven. But until then, we are called to participate with God in the fulfillment of a life dream…His plan for us.

So as the leaving phase closes, another one begins: the famine phase.

Genesis 12:10 says, "Now there was a famine in the land, and Abram went down to Egypt to live there a while because the famine was severe." How heartbroken Abram must have been to leave all that was comfortable and move to the land where God promised to fulfill his dreams, only to have to pack up and move away because of a severe famine.

During such a disappointing passage, your roots grow deeper, not just wider. Don't second-guess what God is doing. Rather, look for ways to dig deeper into His Word, His character, and His faithfulness in this time. Growing deep roots isn't easy. Skimming the shallow dirt of the surface and growing outward is much easier, but roots that grow outward do not anchor the tree and sustain its growth through the years. Isaiah 61:3 says, "They will be called oaks of righteousness, a planting of the LORD for the display of his splendor."

During the time of famine we will have to dig deep, drawing our sustenance from God's Word. Not one of our biblical heroes escaped the famine phase before being used by God in a mighty way. Noah left to get on the ark and then had to endure the flood. Ruth left the banquets of Moab to glean leftover wheat from someone else's field. David left the gentle sheep to face the fierce Goliath. The disciples left with Jesus only to discover He was not going to be an earthly king but rather a crucified Savior. Abraham experienced a physical famine but also a dream famine as well.

God Is Faithful in the Famine

God had promised to make Abraham the father of a great nation, yet Abraham's wife, Sarah, had been unable to conceive. How heartbroken Abraham and Sarah must have been to have God plant in their hearts this amazing dream of a family, only to watch the years tick by with no children to call their own.

So Abraham went to God and shared his distress. Have you gone to God and poured your heart out to Him? Remember, this journey will be a lot less about the places He eventually takes you and much more about the relationship He establishes with you along the way. He wants us to communicate with Him every day through every thought, every step, every victory, every defeat, every question, and every assurance.

In Genesis 15:5-6 God repaints the vision for Abraham, assuring him that it *will* come to pass, and gives him a visual illustration of how big God's dreams for us are. God took Abraham outside and said, "Look up at the heavens and count the stars—if indeed you can count them...so shall your offspring be."

Wow! What a picture. What a destiny. What a big promise. And verse 6 includes a sentence that made my heart jump. Abraham had been walking in obedience since God called him, but he never proclaimed that he actually believed God's dream for him. But this is where he is credited, not for doing something, but for establishing deep in his heart that God was to be trusted because Abraham knew that He would be faithful. "Abram believed the LORD, and he credited it to him as righteousness."

Phase 3
Believing and Seeing

After the leaving and the famine time comes the phase where we learn to believe God. We must watch for His beautiful confirmations and divine appointments, for they will be there if we take heed to look for them. We must never allow ourselves to be so distracted by the famine that we miss this wonderful new phase of really believing and letting that belief settle in even the deep recesses of our heart. This believing time is vital, for it will carry us through other tough times to come. It will remind us, assure us, comfort us, and motivate us that God is to be trusted through every circumstance—even the coming death phase.

The Death of the Dream

And then Abraham experienced the death phase shortly after God finally blessed him with his long-awaited son, Isaac. Probably when Isaac was about to become a teenager, God called Abraham to give him up. The dream was just about to be fully realized, and now death loomed on the horizon. Genesis 22:2 says, "Then God said, 'Take your son, your only son, Isaac, whom you love, and go to the region of Moriah. *Sacrifice him there* as a burnt offering on one of the mountains I will tell you about.'"

I fully believe that God had Abraham walk through this shocking test of obedience to see which came first—his dream or his God. We are tempted to give a quick answer and move past this uncomfortable question without giving it the thought it deserves. This is serious business to God. We quickly take possession of our hopes and dreams, and we don't want to ever give them back. Like a self-centered two-year-old, we scream, "Mine. Mine. Mine!" God can never let that be the cry of our hearts. Our heart must beat in tandem with His. The only way for that to happen is for us to constantly take our dream to Him with open hands and willingly declare, "Yours. Yours. Yours!" Abraham's dream to be the father of a great nation was God's dream first. God is the author of your dream as well. But He's not just the author of the dream, He's the perfecter as well (Hebrews 12:2). Our job is not to figure it all out, manipulate it into being, make the contacts, guard it fiercely, and stake an unwavering claim on it. God started it. God is faithful and more than able. God will finish it.

The Lord Will Provide

"Early the next morning Abraham got up and saddled his donkey. He took with him two of his servants and his son Isaac" (Genesis 22:3). Abraham did not hesitate. He believed God even to the point of death. He got up early and made God's command the priority of the day. I'm sure though his feet walked obediently, his heart ached for reassurance. Somewhere along the journey to the mountain, I believe God gave him assurance that He had it under control and that Abraham could trust Him completely. As Abraham left to take Isaac up to the altar, he says something very surprising to the servants being left behind, "We will worship and then _we_ will come back to you" (Genesis 22:5).

How did Abraham know that both he and Isaac would return? Was it just wishful thinking? Was he just trying to protect the servants from the terrifying truth? Or did he trust that if God allowed the dream to die, He could certainly resurrect it as well? God provided a ram as the sacrifice for Abraham, and He provides it for each one of us as well.

> So Abraham called that place "The LORD Will Provide." And to this day it is said, "On the mountain of the LORD it will be provided." The angel of the LORD called to Abraham from heaven a second time and said, "I swear by myself, declares the LORD, that because you have done this and not withheld your son, your only son, I will surely bless you and make your descendents as numerous as the stars in the sky and as the sand on the seashore. Your descendents will take possession of the cities of their enemies, and through your offspring all nations on earth will be blessed, because you have obeyed me" (Genesis 22:14-18).

Only God can give such a dream, and only God can bring it to pass.

Resurrection

The final phase, which we will more fully explore in chapters 17–20, is the glorious resurrection. It is the fulfillment of that which God has promised and brought about Himself. Our greatest satisfaction will come when we stand in awe at what God accomplishes as we simply walk in faith.

How appropriate for Abraham's dream of a great nation and for our dreams as well. "And to this day it is said, 'On the mountain of the LORD it will be provided'" (Genesis 22:14).

Personal Bible Study

1. Read Acts 7:1-8.

This is a New Testament account of the story of Abraham. This sermon, preached by Stephen just before he was stoned, is the longest recorded in Acts. Why do you think Stephen takes the time to recount Israel's history to his audience? What is his objective in reminding the people of these stories of their past?

2. As the Christian church is growing, Stephen reminds the Jews of their covenant relationship with God. By reminding them of the faith of their forefathers, he is also bringing to mind the patriarchs' response to God's call on their lives. What was their response?

3. Now read Genesis 12:4-9.

What was Abram's response to God?

Write down in your notebook the verse that best states Abram's response to God. Is this your response to God as well?

4. If you are ready, write a prayer to God claiming this verse as your response to Him. Be sure and record the date that you prayed this prayer. Be prepared for what God will do in your life if you pray this prayer!

5. Read Proverbs 18:24; John 15:13-15; James 2:23.

God longs to hear our prayers. He wants to pull us up into His lap and hear about our day, our grief, our victories. Something happens through this process of pouring out our hearts to Him. As we commune with Him and depend on Him, we grow closer to Him. He truly becomes our Friend. He wants to be the *first* one we turn to when our hearts are broken, the one we go to seeking wisdom for a problem, and the one to give us a big thumbs-up when we are victorious. He is our Comforter and our Counselor, available 24 hours a day, just a prayer away. We can derive much confidence from implementing this truth into our prayer lives. Because he had a relationship with God that was based on faith, Abraham was called God's friend. We have the same opportunity today. What a Friend we have in Jesus, indeed.

6. Read Jeremiah 31:31-33.

I heard a Bible teacher once say that this verse was God's phone number! God has issued a new covenant with us through salvation. It is an everlasting, unchanging covenant initiated by God because of His great love for us. All that He asks for is obedience on our part. We do not have to be brave or smart or witty. We don't even need to know exactly where we are going—just whom we are following. Will you step out as Abraham did—with a new name and a new heart, one that desires to follow God every step of the way, leaving the familiar, the comfortable in search of God's best for you? Write down what you feel God is calling you to leave and ask Him to help you take steps away from these things.

PHASE TWO

Famine

Five

The Adventure Our Souls
Were Made For

WE HAVE EXPERIENCED THE LEAVING PHASE, and we've stepped out with God. Unfortunately, we aren't immediately ushered to the land of great promise and dreams fulfilled. This new place is dusty, unfamiliar, and unexpected. This is where the dry, barren, uncomfortable famine begins. In this new place of sacrifice and surrender, God will take you outside your comfort zone, and you'll learn to depend on Him like never before.

It was a hot day inside and outside at the orphan village in Liberia. The soaring temperatures were inescapable, but at least outside there was a breeze. The boys playing soccer in the field didn't seem to mind the heat because the constant excitement of the game kept them plenty distracted. The 12 boys inside, practicing their choir music, found their eyes wandering often over to the soccer field, where the promise of fun and the cheers of their friends tugged at them. Was membership in the boys' choir worth sacrificing their free time playing soccer?

They were feeling the pain of surrendering to their calling, sacrificing their time, and stepping out of their comfort zone. The famine of fun was hitting them hard. But the 12 boys determined the choir was worth the sacrifice, and they stayed true to the task at hand. Other boys had come and gone from the choir, deciding to satisfy their immediate desires for fun instead of staying true to this calling. And a calling it was.

Liberia had been ravaged by a civil war that left more than 25,000 orphans to be cared for. One of the men called to this daunting task was Pastor Kofi. To raise money and support for the hundreds of orphans in his care, Pastor Kofi had his oldest son form an a cappella boys' choir. This choir was to travel throughout the country of Liberia and perform in churches to solicit support. Little did Pastor Kofi or the boys who signed up to be in the choir know that their vision was way too small. God had a plan that these boys could never have imagined.

A Step of Faith

A woman from the American embassy attended one of the choir's Liberian concerts. Her heart was stirred, and she determined to help the boys get the necessary paperwork completed to be able to come to America. Through this woman's relentless determination and God's divine intervention, the boys were headed to the United States for a concert tour.

Once there, God continued to work miracles. He brought a businessman forward to manage the choir and book concerts. Soon, they were scheduled to sing at more than 130 churches throughout the southeast. Through the concerts, they were able to raise awareness and prayer support for their home country and enough money to feed and care for the many children back in the orphanages for that entire year.

The boys in the choir had made great sacrifices, giving up their favorite time of the day playing soccer to practice their singing. The only promise they had was that they would have a chance to tour around their home country of Liberia to encourage the people in churches. But oh, how God blessed their sacrifice! Little did they know that their step of faith to honor God would result in their biggest dreams coming true.

Dreams Come True

Amazing things happened to each of the boys in that choir. One boy was named Seebo. When I first saw Seebo sing, I was struck that he didn't seem to be singing to the crowd of people in front of him. No, his head was tilted and his eyes focused on the only "Daddy" Seebo had ever known—his heavenly Father. The big voice trumpeting from his small frame poured out songs of joy and hope and peace and love. Though his life circumstances had been void of the things that bring joy, hope, peace, and love to most children, these qualities were evident in his life because God reigned so richly in his heart.

Seebo's joy wasn't a temporary happiness that comes on sunny days and then quickly fades. His hope wasn't based on a bright future. His hope was rooted in Jesus and Jesus alone. His heart was filled with peace and love even though he didn't have a warm bed in a nice home with parents who tucked him in with a prayer and a kiss each night. He had no home or parents to call his own, but he knew God was his Father and he had a home in heaven. He also knew that God answers the prayers of His children, so he prayed that God would make a way for him to find a mommy and daddy.

Meanwhile, David and Debbie were living a great life. David had just been promoted to CEO of a major Fortune 500 company. Debbie was the women's ministry director in one of the fastest-growing churches in her city. They'd just sent their second son off to college, and the time had come for them to do those things they'd waited for. They had plans to travel more and finish decorating their house, and Debbie was going to go back to school for a counseling degree. They were both gifted speakers and teachers and considered using these gifts in some kind of ministry together.

All of that came to a screeching halt when God brought Seebo and his friend into David and Debbie's life through the concert tour. Instantly, David and Debbie fell in love with these two boys and prayerfully decided to adopt them. After these boys settled in, David and Debbie kept hearing them talking about their brothers, sisters, and a special friend still in the orphanage. Soon, this empty-nest couple became the proud parents of eight children—two biological and six adopted from Liberia.

Faith in the Famine

Little Seebo had been a forgotten child in a third-world, war-torn country. But he was a boy who prayed, stayed strong in his faith, and was obedient to walk through every open door before him, and so the orphan became the son of one of the most influential and powerful businessmen in America. Do we serve a big God with big plans or *what?* Rest assured, my friend, the same extraordinary God is looking for faithful people through whom He can reveal His extraordinary purposes and ways.

Seebo's story issues a challenge to us all. The more we really believe the truths God calls us to believe, the more we will take chances with God. We can press through the pains of the famine and find comfort in knowing that God has a good plan even in our discomfort. Yet most of us sit in the dust of famine and cry out for comfort and security. We may even turn back to the mud puddles we left behind. All the while, ahead of us are the pure rushing waters our souls were designed to dive into. A sweet place of complete trust in God, great faith, and dreams come true is out there. And inside of us something calls us to dive in and experience the riches of the deep. Something in us wants to believe that God could have great things in store for us too.

Now, think back for a minute to the seemingly ordinary day when Seebo decided to give up his soccer to come inside and join the choir. Do you think he had any idea that this decision of obedience and sacrifice would one day lead to his biggest dreams coming true? Could he have possibly known that he would profoundly affect many other children's futures as well? Sadly, I think about the multitude of Christians who have decided they'd rather be comfortable and play games than get on with the adventure our souls were made for—living a life that requires faith.

A Life that Requires Faith

A life that requires very little faith is not a life that God will use. When we are willing to embark on a life that *requires* faith, we are more aware of God and His ability to provide for us in every detail of our lives. We won't wait until everything in our lives is in order and then decide, *Okay, now I have time to work on living by faith.* We will *never* have everything in order, and faith can't be dispensed like a can of soda from a machine. Faith is learned through life. Through the messy and unpredictable everyday events that often stumble us, we become aware of our desperate need for God. I have determined that once I leave the mud puddles of the past, I'll not look back regardless of how hard the famine gets. I'll focus on what is ahead and find joy in knowing God always comes through.

Let's play a simple game. Without looking, can you name whose face appears on the one-dollar bill, the five-dollar bill, and the ten-dollar bill? I recently posed this question to more than a thousand people in a church service. I then told them to raise their hand if they could say without a shadow of a doubt all three answers. The crowd looked around to see only three people out of a thousand raise their hands. Odd, isn't it? These bills pass through our hands on a daily basis, and yet we live our lives so unaware. Did you know the answers?

Washington, Lincoln, and Hamilton, in that order.

The point isn't that we should pay more attention to money. The point is that we must get to the place where we pay more attention to God at work in our daily lives. If we live our lives unaware of God in the small things, we're probably living unaware of His presence in the big things as well. How vitally important it is for us to surrender our hearts to God and ask Him daily to reveal His plans and perspectives to us so we don't miss His activity and His glorious plans for our future.

Look for God's activity around you each day. Your outlook will change, your faith will take on a fresh excitement, and you'll start walking toward the amazing places God is so excited to lead you to.

Personal Bible Study

1. Read Psalm 15; 24:3-6.

Are you ready to climb God's hill so that you can get closer to Him? These two psalms reveal some of the character qualities God looks for in His people. Though these qualities are not possible in our fleshly nature, with God we can aspire to be righteous because He is at work within us. In your notebook, note particular areas you would like to work on throughout this study. Perhaps you have a friend or someone in your group that you could ask to hold you accountable. Above all, remember that this list is here to inspire you, not to overwhelm you or condemn you.

2. Read 1 Samuel 16:7.

God looks at your heart for Him most of all. How quick we are to condemn ourselves and think we can never measure up! God sees you trying. He knows when you are doing the best you can. He saw those young men in Africa make the choices they did, and He honored and blessed their choices. Of course, we can all work on our character and our actions as we constantly seek to become more like Christ. But we must also give Him time to work on us from the inside out, molding and shaping our hearts according to His design. What are some heart issues you need to ask for God's help in working on? Do you harbor unforgiveness toward someone? Is a secret sin haunting you? Are you bitter toward someone who does not meet your expectations? Pour out your heart to the Lord in your notebook. Ask Him to reveal the truth to you, ask Him to cleanse your heart, and pray for wisdom and courage to do what He tells you to do.

3. Read 2 Chronicles 1:11; Psalm 119:72; Jeremiah 15:16; Romans 10:1.

What is your heart's delight? Is it God's wisdom and understanding? Do you delight in His Word?

4. Matthew 6:21 says, "Where your treasure is, there will your heart be also." My pastor often reminds us that it is easy to tell where someone's heart lies—just take a look at their checkbook and their calendar. Where does your money go? Where do you spend your time? God longs to be your heart's delight. Psalm 37:4 says, "Delight yourself in the LORD, and he will give you the desires of your heart." Determine to delight yourself in Him, and trust Him to work out the rest.

Six

God's Extraordinary Invitation

PERHAPS YOU READ THE PREVIOUS CHAPTER and thought, *Well, that's an interesting story, but what does it have to do with me?*

Well, let me tell you the rest of the story.

Two of the teenage boys in that choir, Jackson and Mark, had been orphaned as babies when their parents and most of their siblings were killed by rebel forces. Those babies, along with so many others, were brought to the orphanage and were taught how to pray, how to have faith in the face of extreme adversity, and, despite times of starvation and deadly attacks by the rebels, how to keep God's joy dancing in their hearts.

Night after night these boys knelt beside their makeshift beds and poured out prayers of thanksgiving and hope that one day they'd hear six simple yet life-changing words, "You are my child— welcome home." Though they couldn't always see God's hand at work, they trusted His heart and rejoiced in the simplest of blessings each day.

God had a perfect design for their prayers to be answered and worked miracle after miracle to bring these boys to America.

But little did I realize that Art and I were to be part of the answer to those boys' prayers. Our life was busy and full, and we were enjoying being the parents of three little girls. So you can imagine my surprise the night I went to the boys' choir concert at our church, only to have our family's life changed forever.

Moved and Terrified

I remember as I sat in the concert that night that from out of nowhere, God whispered to my heart that two of those boys singing in the front of the church were mine. *Right,* I thought. *Sure.*

I felt like sticking my fingers in my ears and singing, *La, la, la, la, la...I'm not listening to You, Lord!* But my song didn't deter the Lord, and the assurance seemed to grow more certain. I decided to try a new tactic with Him. *Lord, I just came here tonight to bring my girls to a simple little cultural event. I'm not looking for a major life change. My life is already very full with speaking and writing and homeschooling three girls. We don't do BOYS in our house. We "think pink," and my husband is okay with that. Besides, all my friends would think I was crazy, and my husband would never think this is a good idea.*

God wasn't discouraged by my response. As a matter of fact, His stirring in my heart grew more and more intense as the evening went on. After the concert, I asked one of their directors which of the boys still needed homes (just so that I could pray for them). He told me that eight of the twelve boys still needed to find families to adopt them. He encouraged me to walk into the reception area where the boys were greeting people. If God intended for some of these boys to be ours, he was sure I would know it.

I rather reluctantly walked into the reception area, and in a matter of seconds, two boys, Jackson and Mark, walked up to me, wrapped their arms around me, and called me *Mom.* I was moved and terrified at the same time.

How could I call Art and drop this bomb on him? I wouldn't even consider bringing home a new *pet* without talking extensively with him, so how was I to explain that two boys from halfway across the world are calling me Mom?

We were the last family to leave the concert. My girls and I hugged the boys goodbye and started making our way home. I flipped open my cell phone and with trembling hands called Art.

How? Why?

For several weeks, we cried out to God, desperate for His guidance and wisdom. We talked to our friends and our parents, and most of them did think we were more than a little crazy. We pondered every aspect and wrestled with this decision deep in our spirits. Art's questions centered more on the *how* aspects. How could we financially increase the size of our family? How would we find the time in our already crammed schedule? How would we raise boys? How could we protect our girls? How would we find room in our home? The list went on and on with a host of other *how* questions.

My deepest questions centered more on the *why. Why us?* I'm not even sure I do this motherhood thing right with just three kids, much less five! I want to be a great mom, but sometimes I just get tired, frustrated, angry, and out of sorts. *God, shouldn't You call someone who looks a little more like the Old Woman in the Shoe and who can handle loads of kids with a smile?*

Then there's the whole perfection thing. I like my house to be neat, tidy, and quiet. This has been doable with three girls—but boys are loud and messy, especially teenage boys. And finally, I'm busy. Lord, You've blessed me with a ministry that's grown beyond my wildest imagination. I travel and speak, and I don't feel You calling me to give that up. But it's not humanly possible to add two more children and continue with my calling, is it? Why me, Lord? Why me?

Heaven Sent

I called my dear friend Sheila one day and asked her this question. I poured out my heart. I unloaded all my doubts and questions. She patiently listened without much response. "Why me, Sheila? Why me?" Then quietly and prayerfully she answered. "Because God knew you'd say yes, Lysa."

I was stunned. It was the highest compliment I'd ever received. My heart was filled with joy as suddenly memories filled my mind of the years of spiritual training God had taken me through to get me to the place where I could be called a woman who says yes to God.

There were other confirmations for me and for Art. One came when we were on a plane traveling together to speak at a marriage conference. We were having one of our "Are we crazy?" discussions when a woman from the row behind us approached our seat and leaned in to speak with us. She told us that God had been prompting her for more than an hour to say something to us, but she was nervous about intruding into our conversation. We smiled and reassured her that we'd like to hear what she had to say. She went on to tell us that she and her husband had three daughters when God called them to adopt some foreign children, and God wanted us to know that everything would be all right. As she turned to leave, she handed me her business card, which had the words printed across the top: Heaven Sent.

God's Finale

When we returned home from that trip, we asked the boys' director if we could schedule one of their final concerts at our home church. Many of my friends thought we were crazy, so I thought they might be more understanding if they heard what I heard that first night as these precious boys sang of the joy of the Lord. I also thought the visit might help give our boys an easier transition into the church body. But God had a grander design for the evening in mind.

The night was magical—one of the last concerts of their tour. They'd sung in more than 130 churches and raised enough money to feed all their friends back home in the orphanage in Liberia for a year. Their mission had been a great success, but six of the boys still needed homes. They needed a miracle. And a miracle is exactly what God had designed for that night. Those friends who thought we were so crazy are now proud parents of Liberian boys!

People lined up at the end of the program to get to know the boys, and we had more willing families than boys to adopt. All of the rest of those boys found parents that night, and at the writing of this book, more than 22 kids (siblings and friends of the boys) from the Liberian orphanage have now been adopted by families in our church.

David and Debbie Alexander, mentioned in the previous chapter, really had their doubts when we first told them of our decision to adopt. They thought what we were doing was commendable, but taking teenage boys into a family of only young girls? Yes, they thought we were crazy. But Debbie came to that concert that night and then she understood. Recently Debbie wrote me to thank me for being crazy, for it led to their *six* new blessings!

Just Say Yes

Now think back to me sitting in that church pew, just going about my ordinary life when God's extraordinary invitation burst forth. I could have so easily walked out of that church and ignored God's stirring. I've done that more times than I'd like to admit. But look at everything we would have missed out on had I done that. This recent photo tells it all.

God has truly blessed our obedience. From left to right: Jackson, Hope, Lysa (with Champ!), Art, Brooke, Ashley, and Mark.

My involvement in God's perfect design began with one simple answer: *Yes. Yes, God, I will embrace what You have for me. Though it's hard and doesn't even seem to make sense, I will embrace it as Your perfect design because Your ways are higher than my ways!*

Last night, we had the privilege to tuck five blessings from God into bed. Jackson and Mark said their prayers, and our eyes filled with tears when they thanked God for answering all those many years of prayer and helping them find their way home. We had all experienced the awesome embrace of God as He brought our family together in a way only He could.

What a picture for our orphaned souls. That's what we all were until many centuries ago the cries of a newborn baby proclaimed that our King, our Savior, our Lord of Lords, our Prince of Peace, Jesus Christ was born. Then He lived and loved and submitted to death on a cross. Three days later, death was defeated as Jesus rose from the dead and became the way for our longing hearts to hear those six simple yet life-changing words: "You are my child—welcome home."

That's what God says to all who trust in Him and accept Jesus Christ as Lord of their life.

Let me encourage you that your spiritual journey doesn't end the minute you become a Christian—that's where it really begins! Being a follower of Christ is a continual process of learning, growing, stretching, and trusting. Each day we can look and listen for God's invitation to join Him in His wondrous work. It was never part of my plan to have more children, but praise God, it was part of His plan.

Look for the Joy

Has it been easy? No. I left my comfort zone and entered into a famine place where I am forced to depend on God like never before. Are there some days I feel like tearing my hair out and wish I had less laundry, less messes, lower grocery bills, and more "me" time? Yes. But this life is not about me. It's about joining hands with Jesus to fulfill whatever tasks He sets before me and to share His love with all He brings my way. Don't miss this point—though the famine phase is hard, it does not have to be void of joy. Look for the joy. It is there. Answered prayers, treasures of wisdom, and the peace of God's provision are waiting for you in this phase. Depending on God brings such joy as I would never know any other way.

For example, our three daughters have grown more spiritually this past year than I could have ever imagined. They aren't just reading about loving others, they are living it. They've adjusted wonderfully. And my ministry? Adopting these boys has taken me away from the ministry quite a bit, but God has grown the ministry more this year than ever before. Had I not adopted the boys, I could have worked hours on end trying to make things happen, but I could never have accomplished what has come from God's hand.

I'm convinced breakthroughs come during this famine phase, not when we're striving to make them happen. Breakthroughs happen when we get about the business of honoring God moment by moment, step-by-step, day by day by what we do and, more importantly, with the thoughts we think *while* we do. People who don't say yes to the Lord can still live a good life. But only those who fully embrace God can experience the wonder and awe of a "yes" heart that lives the *great* life He intends.

What is God calling you to do His way today? You may never be called to adopt children from a foreign land, but God is calling you, wooing you, pursuing you, inviting you to something richer with Him. May your ordinary be invaded with His extraordinary invitation to press through the famine phase and to live life His way!

Personal Bible Study

1. Read Psalm 37:5; Proverbs 16:3.

Is God calling you to something big—really big? Is it bigger than you could ever accomplish on your own? Note in your notebook what is stirring in your heart.

2. It's time to commit whatever God is laying on your heart to Him. Lay your burdens, anxieties, fears, and misgivings on Him, and let Him take care of the details. He is your Father, and He wants to help you work it out. Write a prayer, laying down your burdens and asking for the Father's help.

3. Read Matthew 6:25-27; 1 Peter 5:7.

When you're embarking on an adventure with God, it's easy to get bombarded by all the "what ifs" of the task at hand. I know Art and I dealt with our share of these when we were considering our adoption. We had our own fears, our well-meaning friends and family expressed their doubts, and Satan added his insistent whisperings. Instead of looking at the impossibilities of the adoption, we ultimately decided to step out in faith according to what we knew God was telling us to do. When doubt began to take root, we depended on God to work out the unknowns. We returned to the throne room many times to cast our cares on Him. We knew we served a big God who could handle all that we had to cast upon Him. He took it all and—as I shared—worked out every detail. He put to rest every fear. Record one way God has already started putting your fears to rest through some confirmation from Him.

4. Read Jeremiah 6:16; Mark 10:21-22.

When God calls, not everyone says yes. These two passages give us glimpses of those who decided not to take a great adventure with God. What do you think stopped them?

5. It would have been so easy for me to get up the night of the concert, leave the church, and pretend I had never heard from God. Likewise, the Liberian boys would all still be back in Liberia had they not accepted God's invitation to join Him in His work. How many of us have divine appointments with the God of the universe but ignore them because we are paralyzed by our fear of the unknown? What is stopping you or has stopped you in the past?

God holds the future in His hands. Spend time in prayer asking God what your next step is (not the whole plan). You may want to write down your prayer in your notebook. Proverbs 23:18 says, "There is surely a future hope for you, and your hope will not be cut off."

Seven

God Is with You

WHEN ART AND I WERE STRUGGLING about whether or not to adopt Mark and Jackson, we continued to look for confirmations from God. Many confirmations came, and we decided to proceed with the adoptions without doubt. We trusted that God was with us and that He would work everything out. But one thing kept nagging at me: How in the world will I fit two more lives into my already busy schedule? Do I give up being in ministry? Do I give up homeschooling? Do I give up writing?

I was smack-dab in the middle of a famine, and though I knew the purpose was to learn to depend on God like never before, it was hard. The more I prayed about and pondered trying to make everything fit, the more I kept saying, "There's no way…there's just no way." I wasn't feeling led to give up anything in my busy life, which made no sense. *Something* had to give. So I continued to pray and watch for God's answer. I would stop trying to figure it all out and simply wait for God.

Jesus Is the Way

A few weeks later I flew to California to teach at a women's retreat. I prayed off and on the entire four-hour plane ride and two-hour drive to the retreat center. I kept looking for some kind of assurance from God that He was hearing my prayers and that He knew my struggle. When I arrived at the retreat center without that assurance, I was disappointed. I would be ministering to the ladies. The time had come for me to give, not to receive…or so I thought.

I walked to the registration desk to check in, and the woman behind the counter handed me a name badge. Every woman was being given a name badge with her name on it along with a name for God from the Bible. When I glanced down at my tag, I was shocked. The name of God I'd been given was The Way. For days, I'd been telling God there was *no way*, and now He was reminding me that there is *always* a way with Him.

In John 14:5 Thomas asks, "Lord we don't know where you are going, so how can we know the way?" What a great question. Like me, you may have asked this many times, especially during the famine phase. You've stepped out of your comfort zone and you feel uncertain, so now what? In the next verse Jesus tells us plainly, "I am the way and the truth and the life. No one comes to the Father except through me."

Thomas had just asked Jesus the way to heaven, but in an even deeper spiritual sense, he was asking the way to assurance. Jesus' answer was good enough for Thomas, and it's good enough for us as well. Jesus is the way, our certain path in life, our way out of the famine. He is the truth, God's promises made real. And He is the life—the only way to live with purpose now and the only way to receive life eternal.

New Wineskins

We must expand our vision. In our own strength, achieving our dreams may be impossible. But with God, there is a way! We must begin thinking in a new way—His way. In Matthew 9:17 Jesus says, "Neither do men pour new wine into old wineskins. If they do, the skins will burst, the wine will run out and the wineskins will be ruined. No, they pour new wine into new wineskins, and both are preserved."

In biblical times, wine wasn't stored in bottles as it is today. It was put into wineskins made of leather that had been dried and cured and formed to hold the wine. Joel Osteen makes this observation:

> When the wineskins were new, they were soft and pliable, but as they aged, they often lost their elasticity; they wouldn't give anymore. They would become hardened and set, and they couldn't expand. If a person poured new wine in an old wineskin, the container would burst and the wine would be lost . . . That lesson is still relevant today. We are set in our ways, bound by our perspectives and stuck in our thinking. God is trying to do something new, but unless we are willing to change, unless we are willing to expand and enlarge our vision, we'll miss His opportunities for us.[1]

I can live with my limited vision, convinced that there is no way and overcome with uncertainty in my time of famine, or I can take God's hand and confidently proclaim Him to be my way. I wish I could impress you with my great organizational skills that allow my life to flow seamlessly, but I can't. I plan and I delegate, but I rely daily on God to fill in my many gaps. I am amazed that God so freely gives His help when I ask for it. We all need help to get through our times of famine, so ask Him to help you.

God constantly reminds me of details I've forgotten. He sends people who are available to help me. He goes before me and arranges carpools and schedules in a way that shocks me. When I sit down to plan out my weeks with my husband, I'm always amazed that each week works. But I really shouldn't be because God is truly the way.

God wants you to succeed in His plans. Do you really believe that? Have you changed your thinking enough to trust that to be true? You can't go on this grand adventure with God and keep your old way of thinking. Remember, we've left that behind in the last section. Like the wine, you must have a new wineskin—a new pattern of thinking for this new way of living. Remember, the purpose of this famine phase is for you to learn to depend on God like never before.

Art and I aren't the only ones who had adjustments to make. Our boys have had to make them as well. In order to step into this new life God offered them, they had to leave all that was familiar back in Liberia. And when they left, they did not step immediately into their promised land. They progressed through each of the phases of faith when they joined our family. In their famine phase, they realized that life in America is not nearly as laid-back and relaxed as life in Africa, especially at school. They have a lot of catching up to do.

Moving Mountains

Jackson has always been an eager learner, so the transition hasn't been as difficult for him. Mark, however, would just as soon forget about school. Sometimes education looks to him like a huge overwhelming mountain that will only be moved by the miraculous hand of God. He even prays for God to work a miracle and drop the knowledge he needs into his brain. Though he is a bright kid, reading, writing, and arithmetic are very challenging at times.

I'm Mark's primary teacher, and I must admit that I too have prayed for God to move this mountain of knowledge right into Mark's brain! The Bible tells us in Matthew 17:20, "I tell you the truth, if you have faith as small as a mustard seed, you can say to this mountain, 'Move from here to there' and it will move. Nothing will be impossible for you." Some people read this verse and get frustrated because even though they have faith, the mountains don't seem to be moving. Such was the case with Mark. Though he was believing and trying, the mountain didn't seem to be moving.

So Mark decided to try going around the mountain. The next time I gave him a math test, he scored a whopping 100 percent! But his answer to the last problem included a note from the answer key to the teacher. How my heart broke as I realized he'd cheated.

Though we forgave him and made him retake the math test, his punishment needed to be a visual reminder that God can move the educational mountain. Art had Mark move a huge pile of rocks a short distance from one spot to another spot. The rocks were heavy and could only be moved one at a time. He worked for a long while and felt frustrated that he'd hardly made any progress. But several hours later, he stood back amazed. The mountain had been moved. Though God could have instantaneously moved it, He chose another way. He gave Mark the strength to move it one rock at a time.

Yes, faith still moves mountains. But sometimes the greater act of faith is not praying for the mountain to move instantly but rather hanging in there while God helps you to move it bit by bit.

During this famine phase, many people are tempted to doubt and sometimes even give up. Maybe we heard God wrong. Maybe God isn't with us. The doubts bombard us and steal our passion to press on. When this happens, we are looking at the entire mountain and losing sight of the part God wants to help us move today. Don't try to make your whole dream come true at once. Just fulfill the small part of the mission He's asking you to do today. Just carry that one rock. Ask God, *What is my assignment for today?* Do that part and be satisfied that God is pleased. Be encouraged and continue to press on!

Personal Bible Study

1. Read 2 Samuel 22:29-46; Philippians 4:13.

God's way is perfect. We may not understand His plan, but we know we can trust it to be better for us than anything we could devise for ourselves. God sees the big picture—beyond the famine time and all the way to the promised land. Our limited vision is finite and unreliable. The more we realize this, the more we know that we are better off depending on God. Second Samuel 22 shows us what we can do with God's help. Read through this list a few times. What do you need God to help you accomplish right now? Write down your answer and ask God to show how you can experience the same type of victorious Christian living that David is describing. Second Samuel 22:31 says, "As for God, His way is perfect; the word of the LORD is flawless." God showed me that He is the Way. Let Him show you that too through His Word.

2. Read Judges 21:25; Isaiah 53:6.

We can easily forget that Jesus is the way, choosing to go our own way instead. Though these are both Old Testament passages, they definitely still hold true today. God is loving and patient with us, His rebellious children who stubbornly try to do things *our* way. Isaiah tells us "each of us has turned to his own way." Without exception, every one of us is included in that verse. We allow our pride, our independence, and our sin nature to get us off the path of God's way and onto a path that leads us to less than God's best. We take our eyes off God and do what is best in our own eyes. In this time of famine, Satan comes to tempt us to go his way. He makes following him look enticing and easier than God's way—a shortcut. Just remember that God's way may not include shortcuts, but it does lead to success by God's design, which will never disappoint (Romans 5:3-5a). Meditate on these verses and record your thoughts in your notebook.

3. Read Proverbs 16:3; 2 Corinthians 6:4-10.

Godly success and worldly success rarely look the same. In God's economy everything is upside down from the way the world sees things. That's because we live in a fallen world run by the prince of this world, Satan. Satan wants us to believe that second best just doesn't cut it, but God says, "The last will be first, and the first will be last" (Matthew 20:16). As we hope to realize godly success, may we strive to understand exactly what godly success even looks like. Using the concordance of your Bible, look up the word "success" or "succeed" and find out what God has to say about success. Remember to keep seeking God in all that you do, and success will follow. Record your verses in your notebook.

Eight

Refusing to Get Bogged Down in Bitterness

I MUST CAUTION YOU NOT TO GET bogged down in bitterness during this famine phase. This is a season of learning to depend on God. As a result, things will be stripped from you that hinder the relationship He wants to have with you. You may experience a shake-up in your finances, your friendships, your position of leadership, your expectations, or one of a thousand other things that we put our trust in. God wants our complete trust. So whenever He strips something away, He does it for our good and not to harm us.

Resist getting bitter with people or circumstances. Take great comfort in knowing this is but a season, it will soon pass, and one day you will actually thank God for taking you through this. This time of loss will lead to a time of great celebration one day.

As we look at the story of Joseph, take courage from one who has gone before you. Put yourself in his shoes. Watch him make the constant decision to honor God during his famine phases, and watch how God restores his life back a hundredfold time and again.

Also, take heed of his brothers in this story and watch how their poor decision to let bitterness consume them hurts them. What will be the story of your famine phase?

Joseph's Leaving Phase

To set the stage, we must remember Abraham from our chapters on leaving. God promised Abraham that he would be the father of a great nation. The only problem was that Abraham and his wife, Sarah, experienced years of infertility. Had Abraham heard God wrong?

No, God just had a much different timetable than Abraham and Sarah had. When the couple was quite old, they were blessed with a son named Isaac. Isaac grew up, married, and had two sons, one of whom was Jacob. Then Jacob grew up, married, and had 12 sons by four different women. His favorite wife bore him his favorite son, and then she died giving birth to a second son. The favored son was Joseph, and his brothers grew to despise him.

Genesis 37:4 says, "When his brothers saw that their father loved him more than any of them, they hated him [Joseph] and could not speak a kind word to him." In this same chapter, verse 11 goes on to state the obvious: "His brothers were jealous of him." The brothers held such bitterness and animosity against Joseph that their hearts became cold and their judgment clouded. One day as they were tending the sheep on a hillside, they saw Joseph coming in the distance and plotted to kill him. The oldest brother stepped in and convinced the others not to kill Joseph but rather to throw him into an empty pit and hold him captive.

Before long some merchants passed by on their way to Egypt, giving the brothers their perfect answer. By selling Joseph, they acquired some money and got rid of their hated brother all in one transaction. They took Joseph's beautiful coat, which had been a gift from their father, shredded it, dipped it in animal's blood, and returned home to break the news to their father that Joseph had been killed by a wild animal.

Meanwhile, Joseph is making a journey of more than 30 days through the desert on foot, chained, and probably treated worse than an animal. After all, he was now merchandise to be sold once he reached Egypt. I can't help but think about how Joseph must have felt during those long hot days and harsh lonely nights. But the Scriptures make clear that God was with Joseph just as He is with all of His wronged and brokenhearted children.

God Was with Him

Joseph finally reaches Egypt and is sold into slavery. His life there sees many ups and downs, trials, tragedies, and triumphs, but God is with him through it all. Whether he was held in captivity by slave traders, serving as a slave, or in prison, the Bible constantly reminds us that the Lord was with Joseph. Genesis 39:2-4 says, "The Lord was with Joseph and he prospered, and he lived in the house of his Egyptian master. When his master saw that the Lord was with him and that the Lord gave him success in everything he did, Joseph found favor in his eyes and became his attendant. Potiphar put him in charge of his household, and he entrusted to his care everything he owned."

Oh, my friend, think of what a bitter person Joseph could have been. He could have claimed his right to charge that he'd been mistreated and abused. He could have let bitterness wrap his heart in a web of anger, anxiety, and revenge, but he didn't. He chose not to. He made the conscious choice to honor God with his actions and his attitudes, and God honored him. Notice also that God didn't immediately pluck him from the situation but rather honored him in the situation. How many times do we ask God to take away an unpleasant circumstance, and He doesn't? Seek to honor him and then remember to look for the ways He's honoring you, not by removing you but by sending blessings to you in that place.

From Prisoner to Prince

And we must not overlook the fact that the people around Joseph observed him honoring the Lord. People are watching you. Even when you think they aren't looking, they are. They want to see if your claims about God's faithfulness hold true even when life gets hard. Joseph's master saw God in Joseph and was drawn to God's Spirit in Joseph. We must remember that our bitterness turns people away. Being filled with God's sweet fragrance of acceptance will attract and bless and, most importantly, draw people to God. Joseph honored God time and time again, and God blessed and honored him in return.

Still, life didn't go as we would hope for Joseph. Potiphar's wife tried to trap him in sin and had him thrown in prison. "But while Joseph was there in prison, the LORD was with him; he showed him kindness and granted him favor in the eyes of the prison warden" (Genesis 39:20-21).

Eventually, Joseph interpreted a dream for Pharaoh. God was warning Pharaoh to prepare for seven years of plenty followed by seven years of famine. Pharaoh was so impressed by God's Spirit in Joseph that he placed Joseph in charge of the entire land of Egypt, second only to Pharaoh himself. Joseph, once a forgotten slave boy, now wielded the power of a king. Ring any bells? God did this for Joseph. He did it for the Liberian boys. And God has done it for you too. You were once a spiritual orphan with no hope, but now you are adopted as a child of the Most High King!

Ordinary Decisions Can Have Extraordinary Effects

Pharaoh wisely heeded Joseph's predictions, and during the seven years of plenty, Egypt diligently saved up grain to be used when famine hit. Sure enough, seven years later, a terrible famine struck the land, and the grain saved the lives of the people.

Jacob and his family were also experiencing extreme famine, and they heard that Egypt had grain. So Jacob sent some of the brothers to Egypt to get some grain to feed their families. The story once again takes many twists and turns, but eventually Joseph recognizes the brothers, has mercy on them, and gives them food, and Jacob's entire family moves to Egypt to live.

All 12 sons of Jacob grow up, marry, raise their families in Egypt, and become the 12 tribes of the nation of Israel. Many years and several generations later, a Pharaoh arose who did not remember Joseph and his great service to Egypt. He was concerned that the very large nation of Israel was a potential threat and could disrupt his powerful Egyptian empire.

Exodus 1:11 says, "So they [the Egyptians] put slave masters over them [the Israelites] to oppress them with forced labor." Verses 12-13 go on to say, "But the more they were oppressed, the more they multiplied and spread; so the Egyptians came to dread the Israelites and worked them ruthlessly." So goes the story of how the entire nation of Israel wound up as slaves in Egypt.

Think back with me to that day many years before when a group of bitter brothers were tending sheep on a very ordinary day and made one tragic decision. They caused harm not only to their family but eventually to the entire nation of Israel. Had they never sold Joseph to be a slave, the nation of Israel would have never wound up as slaves being treated so cruelly in Egypt.

Sadly, those brothers were living their lives very unaware of the tragic consequences that can come from one act of disobedience. The brothers' bitter hearts caused trouble for many on that ordinary day (see Hebrews 12:15). And the effects of their bad decision haunted generations who came after them. As we make ordinary decisions on ordinary days, do we, I wonder, have any idea of the impact and influence those decisions have on the people around us and the generations to come?

All Things Are Possible

Thank God the Liberian boys were aware that with God all things are possible. They didn't get stuck in the bitterness that surely came knocking at the doors of their hearts. After all, their mothers, their fathers, and many of their biological siblings were massacred by evil rebels. Put yourself in their shoes.

You're at home one night with all of your family. Suddenly the front door crashes in, and everyone you love is slaughtered right in front of you. Your home is burned and your money is taken away. Miraculously, you survive, but what future do you have now? You have no money, no one to care for you, nothing. You are taken to an orphanage and left there. You are now a forgotten child in a third-world country.

But God was with those boys. God was with Joseph. And God is most certainly with you too. He has not forgotten you. He knows your circumstances. He knows bitterness has certainly come knocking on your door as well. Don't answer that knock. Don't listen to the voice of bitterness. Don't even crack the door to peek outside. Ask God to slay this unwanted visitor and carry him away. And then you choose daily to never resurrect him.

The decisions you are making today matter. Thank God Joseph was aware that with God all things are possible as he saved the nation of Israel despite being betrayed and hurt by them. What might God have in store for you after the famine? What treasures are you discovering? Have you learned how to depend on God like never before? More importantly, do you have a sure answer settled in your heart that yes, with God, all things are possible?

Personal Bible Study

1. Read Acts 7:9-15.

This passage is a continuation of Stephen's sermon, particularly dealing with the story of Joseph in this section. Notice verse 9 points out that "God was with him." Many times in the Bible, people are described as having God with them. Read Genesis 21:20; 26:3; 39:2; 1 Samuel 18:14; Luke 1:66; and Acts 11:21 for just a few of these references. In these passages, God is clearly *with* those who follow Him. I picture Him walking right beside us as the perfect traveling companion. He walks with us and talks with us and calls us His own, as the old hymn says. How blessed we are to have God as our companion in life. In your notebook, write out one of these verses and record your name in the place of the person's name in the verse. Gain the confidence and strength you need just by knowing that God is with you, just as He was with Joseph and other heroes of the faith.

2. Read Genesis 41:16.

Joseph refuses to take any credit for his success in this verse. He is standing in the presence of the Pharaoh—the most powerful man in the world at that time—who does not worship Joseph's God, yet Joseph is not afraid to give God the glory before Pharaoh. His willingness to glorify God resulted in many blessings for him personally and politically. Read Genesis 41:38-45, and in your notebook, list the blessings God provided for Joseph.

Joseph could have given up, felt betrayed, and turned his back on God when he ended up in Egypt as a slave. Instead he used the opportunity to grow his character and increase his faith all the more. Because of his positive perspective on the situation, he was allowed to see God work out a desperate situation for good. We can have the same perspective according to Romans 8:28 (NKJV): "And we know that all things work together for good to those who love God, to those who are the called according to *His* purpose."

3. Read Genesis 41:50-52.

After Joseph is blessed with his new position as second in command to the Pharaoh, he marries and has two sons named Manasseh and Ephraim. These two sons' names are both significant to Joseph's life, as the verse says. Write in your notebook what the verse says each son's name meant.

4. By the time Joseph married and assumed his new position of leadership, he had spent 13 years in slavery. Was slavery part of God's plan for him? Proverbs 20:24 says, "A man's steps are directed by the LORD." How then can anyone understand his own way?" Joseph knew that God had a plan for his life, and he accepted God's sovereignty regardless of what happened. He knew that God had directed his steps into that pit his brothers had dug for him just as He had directed his steps into a place of power. God had shown Himself faithful from the pit to Potiphar to prison to power. Joseph's sons, in turn, became a living testimony to his conviction that God was with him every step of the way. In your notebook, briefly retrace God's faithfulness through some of the experiences in your life.

PHASE THREE

Believing

Nine

A Most Unlikely Path

ART'S FAMILY LOVES TO GO CAMPING, and I don't mean in a cushy campground with hot showers and power hookups. Oh no, they like a true wilderness, *Survivor* style of camping experience. One where you set up a tent village complete with a makeshift outhouse—a hole in the ground with plastic tarps covering three sides. You can imagine their horror when Art brought Princess, the nickname I have affectionately earned, to participate in the family tradition, pulling an air-conditioned pop-up camper to the remote riverside campsite. They were speechless when their peace and quiet was invaded by the roaring sound of the generator. Then the last straw was when I stepped out of the camper the first morning, having fixed my hair and makeup.

Now in my defense, I met the challenge head-on, and by the end of the week my hair dryer and makeup were things of the past. I even tried bathing in the muddy river like everyone else. I actually enjoyed communing with nature and bonding with my family as we left the modern world behind.

On one of the last days of our adventure, all the kids decided to go swimming in the river. I wasn't concerned in the least as we'd all grown quite comfortable around the water. While they were splashing and laughing their afternoon away, I sat on the bank, delighting in my kids having such a good time with their cousins. Suddenly, something strange caught the corner of my eye. Something was floating on top of the water a short distance from the kids. It appeared to be a stick. There were lots of sticks and other natural debris in and on the water, so I brushed it aside. A few seconds later a question flashed through my mind . . . was it floating or swimming? Sticks don't swim on top of the water—snakes do!

I gasped as one of my worst fears was making its way toward my children. I knew I couldn't panic, so I calmly got all the kids' attention. I told them sternly that it was very important for them to listen to my voice and do exactly as I directed. They needed to get out of the water quickly—but this wouldn't be possible going the normal route toward me. The embankment I was on was too steep, and only one child could slowly climb up at a time. They had to swim across the narrow river to the sandy beach on the other side. Then all the kids could get out of the water quickly, and the men could get the boat between the children and the snake.

I didn't want them to know about the snake and have them panic, so I just said it was very important to do as I was instructing, and they would have a surprise on the other side. The thought of a surprise was all the motivation they needed as they calmly but quickly did exactly as they were told. When the men got to the stick-like creature, they confirmed it was indeed a poisonous snake. Yes, the kids certainly got a big surprise as they realized why it had been so important to make it out of the water, just as I had told them to.

Too Real to Deny

Life is a lot like that snake experience. God knows the best routes for us. He sees dangers and temptations that we don't see along the way. Sometimes we get frustrated with God when He takes us through places we hadn't planned on going. His route sometimes appears to be out of the way, inconvenient, tiresome, and confusing.

But we must recognize His voice, listen carefully, and do exactly as He instructs. My kids did this because they knew me, trusted me, and had been conditioned to obey me.

We must trust God in the same way. When you leave the famine phase, you enter into this wonderful new place of believing God like never before. You've always wanted to believe Him and His promises, and now that you've left your comfort zone and pressed through the pains of the famine, He's become too real to deny.

The longer we walk with God, the more easily we hear His voice and trust His instructions. Throughout Scripture God calls His people "sheep" and refers to Himself as the Good Shepherd. Phillip Keller makes this note in his classic book, *A Shepherd Looks at Psalm 23*:

> In the Christian's life there is no substitute for the keen awareness that my Shepherd is nearby. There is nothing like Christ's presence to dispel the fear, the panic, the terror of the unknown. We live a most uncertain life. Any hour can bring disaster, danger and distress from unknown quarters…Then in the midst of our misfortunes there suddenly comes the awareness that He, the Christ, the Good Shepherd is there. It makes all the difference. His presence in the picture throws a different light on the whole scene. Suddenly things are not half so black nor nearly terrifying. The outlook changes and there is hope…It is the knowledge that my Master, my Friend, my Owner has things under control even when they may appear calamitous. This gives me great consolation, repose and rest.[2]

God Will Help You Want to Obey

Every day the Good Shepherd asks, Do you trust Me? Do you believe Me? Will you follow My commands even when they don't make sense to you? We sheep must give a resounding yes, laying all our own questions aside. God has probably taken you on some unlikely paths before, and you can almost be guaranteed that more lie ahead, so why not make peace with this now? Why not just confirm right out loud that you do trust God and are willing to travel the unlikely paths because you know they are His best?

I challenge you to do this even if you don't feel like it. Feelings follow correct behaviors, not the other way around. Make right choices to honor God, and your feelings will eventually catch up. And though at first following God this way may appear to make your life harder, it actually does the exact opposite. It makes your attitude more in line with His, thus enabling you to weather whatever comes your way.

Though I've tripped and stumbled many times along this most unlikely path with God, He has allowed me to understand what Philippians 2:12-13 means when it instructs, "Continue to work out your salvation with fear and trembling, for it is God who works in you to will and to act according to his good purpose." In other words, it's okay to be scared that you might mess up. It's okay to be honest enough to admit you don't always want to obey. This is human nature. Ask God to help you make wise decisions. Ask Him to help you to *want* to obey. God will work in you to help line your will up with His if only you'll ask.

Have you ever dared to ask this? Have you ever dared to say to God, *Lord, whatever Your will for my life is, that is what I want?* Believing God is not for the weak at heart. It's only for those who want to discover the rich blessings of walking close enough to God to hear the constant drumming of His heartbeat.

God's Heartbeat

I've heard this heartbeat many times. I heard it very clearly on a day that my world could have come crashing in around me. But there it was, thump-thump, thump-thump, thump-thump. So real.

So close. Too close to deny that He was right there with me. So, what could have been a day of devastation was but a bump in the road. I heard His instructions, I did exactly as He told me to do despite my feelings, and He delivered me safely to the other side.

Several months prior to our camping trip, Art told me he wanted to invest our entire life savings in the stock market. A couple of stocks showed great promise, and he wanted to get in on what was sure to be very profitable. I'm not very investment savvy, but I didn't like the sound of putting all our eggs in one basket, so to speak. I voiced my concern but let him do what he thought best.

Then came the day. The day the market crashed. Art came home, and I went to the front door to greet him with some trivial details from the day. The look on his face made me stop speaking. I watched as he slumped down in front me, wrapped his arms around my legs and sobbed, "I've lost it all. Our entire life savings is gone."

Thump-thump, thump-thump, thump-thump. I knew the Lord was close. I knew He would provide. I knew He was allowing this to happen for a reason. He could restore our investment as quickly as He allowed it to go away. Thump-thump, thump-thump, thump-thump. I knew all this, but my flesh screamed out to say, *I told you so! You fool! How could you have done this?* But how could I dishonor God when everything I know about Him reminds me of His constant provision? Did I really think our life savings came from our hard work, or did I know and believe that everything we have comes straight from Him? Thump-thump, thump-thump, thump-thump.

I knelt down in front of Art and cupped his face in my hands. "I loved you yesterday when we had everything. I love you today when we have nothing. I love you, Art, not for what you have but for who you are." This became a marriage-defining moment for us. It was not a path I would have ever freely chosen, but it was the best path. I chose to believe God in this moment. I chose, by the Holy Spirit's power, to honor what I knew to be true about God even though my feelings lagged behind. Now, on the other side of this experience, I can say that what it did for our marriage was priceless. I would have freely given every penny we lost to have what we gained.

God knew best. He always does. Thump-thump, thump-thump, thump-thump.

I had a complete and very unexpected peace. I could have wallowed in what I'd lost and stayed in the hard place of the famine. But something in my soul reached out for God's perspective and grabbed hold of the certainty of His presence, and suddenly I was ushered from famine to believing. The minute I trusted God this way, my famine was over, and I began a new phase of believing God like never before.

You see, in the believing phase your circumstances might not be that much different from what they were in the famine phase. However, the difference is in how you look at them. You have changed. Your outlook has changed. Your belief in God has changed, for you now know this for sure: People may change, and things may change, but God never does. God does not change, and neither do His promises.

Personal Bible Study

1. First read Job 37:1-5; Psalm 29:3-9; and then read 1 Kings 19:11-13; Isaiah 30:21.

In the first set of verses, God's voice is described as a mighty thunder, loud and commanding and awe-inspiring, just as you might expect. In the second set of verses, though, God's voice is quiet and still, barely more than a whisper. I must admit, sometimes I wish I could hear God's voice as loud as thunder so I would know for sure that I had heard Him correctly! But I am grateful that God is gentle with me—whispering His words of affirmation and encouragement. I have learned to listen for the sound of His voice just behind me saying, "This is the way, walk in it." As I take tentative steps forward, I grow more confident in my walk and realize He is with me always.

2. Read 1 Samuel 15:22; Psalm 95:7-8; Hebrews 3:7.

As we learn to listen for God's voice, the next step is to *obey* His voice. These verses show us that God speaks to us with the expectation that we will obey Him as a result. And yet how many of us ignore His voice, argue with His voice, or try to drown out His voice by allowing other noises to fill up our world? As we saw, God's voice is that gentle whisper that can be heard only when we intentionally listen for it. In Psalm 95:7, the original word for "hear" means to *hear with the intention of obeying.* We must take that next step of listening for His voice and then obeying what He has asked us to do. God's Word gives us many examples of how we will miss out on the many blessings He has in store for us if we do not obey His voice, just as the children of Israel missed out on their promised land.

3. Read Psalm 37:23-24; Proverbs 4:11-12; John 11:9.

Sometimes we hear God's voice, and we set out on the path

according to His direction, only to stumble along the way. God's Word warns us that we will stumble from time to time, but He will keep us from falling. James 3:2 says, "We all stumble in many ways." Jesus taught us that we must walk according to God's will. When we are doing that, we have nothing to fear. It is better to walk in obedience than to live in fear of stumbling.

Ten

Roadblocks and Reassurances

WHAT EXACTLY ARE YOU UP TO, GOD? I shook my head in disbelief as I drove slowly down the driveway. I was facing an impossible situation. God was asking me to extend grace to someone who was hurting me. He wanted me to love her when she was doing everything possible to destroy my comfort, my security, and my joy. I felt in no way like honoring God in this moment. I had a whole list of emotions coursing through my body, none of which were loving and kind. But I couldn't shake this overwhelming sense that God was waiting, watching, wooing me to act contrary to my feelings and simply walk in His truth. I was to love this woman who so desperately despised me.

Blockade!

It all started over a dispute about the boundary lines of our property. We soon discovered that indeed we had made a mistake, and part of our driveway was on land that did not belong to us. We tried to buy the small parcel from her to no avail. We tried to reason it out and thought of every scenario possible to fix the problem without having to spend an exorbitant amount of money to dam up part of our pond and move the driveway over. But no solution was acceptable to her, and it became apparent that we'd have to do the least desirable option.

The timing was also a problem. We needed to wait until the dryer summer months when we could drain the pond. But even this was unacceptable, and soon we were greeted by various blockades in our driveway. Huge rocks, sawhorses and boards of wood, and No Trespassing signs blocked our way. Months went by, the blockades got worse, and the less-than-kind letters to us got more frequent. I felt threatened, frustrated, hurt, and bewildered.

Here I was, a woman in a Christian ministry who spends my life teaching women to love one another, and my neighbor couldn't stand the sight of me. I was brokenhearted and rattled, and I began to question myself. Worst of all, I couldn't fix the problem. I cried out to God and begged Him to remove the problem, soften hearts, change minds, or best of all, supernaturally move the driveway. But it was not to be. Week after week, I'd find myself driving down my long winding driveway, only to be halted by the latest blockade attempt.

God's Solution

Then came the day God moved. Not the driveway, and not even the other person's heart. God moved in me. It was the day I came home and found workers building a fence across the drive that would permanently block us from going to and from our home. I was infuriated. How could she do this? Why would she do this? I ran to call someone to help me, someone to rescue me. As I stormed into my home, God suddenly broke through my anger and anxiety and prompted me to take my fence-building adversary a cup of water.

It was a hot summer day, and building a fence is not an easy job. She was tired and thirsty. But the reason she was tired and thirsty was because of all the energy she was exerting to hurt me! Now I was supposed to go give her water to refresh and reenergize her efforts? *God, this is not fair. This does not make sense! She probably won't even take the water I give her.* So this is the place I was in as I slowly made my way down to the fence. As I got out of the car and started toward her, I had to will my feet to walk this obedience path. But then as my arm reached to give her the water, the heaviness lifted, and I so clearly felt God's impression on my heart: *Today it will be physical water, but this is one of the things that will lead to her receiving the living water.*

Her silent stare let me know today was not the day to try and give her the living water, but seeds were planted in her heart and mine. How these seeds will be nurtured is up to the Lord.

Tears filled my eyes as I silently walked back to my car and turned to go back up the driveway. God has the most amazing way to work in the unseen details of life and work out His plan despite our stubbornness. Here I was, kicking and screaming through this situation that I thought seemed so pointless, and all along God had a plan. A plan for her and a plan for me.

Our Assignment

How I wished I could have embraced God's plan sooner than I did. All I could think about was changing the circumstances that were causing me disruption and discomfort. Now I realize that for that season of my life, my assignment from God was to learn to love an enemy. What enemy do you need to love at this moment? Maybe it's a neighbor, a prodigal child, an angry spouse, or an unforgiving friend.

We don't like hard places. Our souls long for the perfection of the Garden of Eden that we were designed for, and yet the world we live in bounces us from one imperfection to the next. Soon we find ourselves empty and exhausted, trying to fix problems that interrupt and inflict pain and heartbreak. We even become frustrated with

God. We know He could fix this problem. With one snap of His holy hand, He could heal the hurts, rearrange the circumstances, restore the broken places, and provide a way out. So why doesn't He?

Growing Up

The answer is that He loves us too much to leave us the way we are. Think about a baby inside his mother's womb. He is warm and well fed. He likes this place of security and safety, but a time comes when he must leave. He must go through the painful shock of being born. It is hard, but if he resists, growth will no longer be possible, and he will die.

Our spiritual life is very much the same. We must continue to grow and embrace God's plans for the life we've been given. We don't grow by changing the adverse circumstances. We grow by embracing God's plans for the circumstances and allowing Him to have His full way in us. Allow Him to work out kinks and imperfections in the core of your soul. Let Him help you find a perspective beyond your own. Only then can you find incredible peace in the storms of life.

The enemies to a great life are not tragedy, heartbreak, and hard times. The enemy to having a great life is to simply lead a good life. A life where you seek comfort and ease above growth. A life where you avoid the risk of taking chances with God. We live in a fallen world, so no one can avoid every pothole in the road of life. *You will have hard times.* You will get bumped and bruised, but you don't have to get bewildered. Say yes to God now. Say yes to whatever He brings your way. Seek Him wholeheartedly through it. Ponder what He is teaching you. Surrender what He is requiring from you. And know that He is working out His wonderful plans for you right now behind the scenes.

Embrace His Plan

This hard place you are in is not a distraction. You are not being sidetracked. This is His way. "'For I know the plans I have for you,' declares the LORD, 'plans to prosper you and not to harm you, plans to give you hope and a future'" (Jeremiah 29:11). You've probably heard this verse quoted time and again, but put it in context with the verses that come after it, and you'll see the call to not only trust God but to have peace in knowing He will carry you through. Verses 12-14 go on to say this:

> "Then you will call upon me and…find me when you seek me with all your heart. I will be found by you," declares the LORD, "and will bring you back from captivity. I will gather you from all the nations and places where I have banished you," declares the LORD, "and will bring you back to the place from which I carried you into exile."

My favorite call to action here is to seek God "with *all* your heart." Not just the parts of your heart crying for ease. Not just the parts of your heart crying for restoration. But find that place in your heart eager for growth, and let it cry out as well. Embrace this perfect plan, and you will find God, see His plan from His perspective, and enjoy peace right in the middle of the storm. In the meantime, my favorite promise here from God is that He will carry us. He carried us into this hard place, this exile of sorts, and He will carry us back out.

This is a season of growth. This is a part of the plan. The road will not be hard all the way through. Continue to call on Him in great confidence, realizing that nothing, no hard place, can separate you from God's comforting presence and boundless mercy. This will soon pass, and on the other side wait rich perspectives, beautiful growth, and yes, stronger faith.

The Rest of the Story

So, whatever happened with the driveway? We had to drain the pond and move the driveway. It broke our heart to see the pond get to such a sad state, and the process of moving the driveway was very expensive. However, God provided every penny we needed to move the driveway in the most surprising ways. Now you can't even see evidences of the great driveway escapade. The barren ground sprouted grass again, and the driveway sits securely on our land. I still pray for my neighbor, who has since moved, and I still hope one day we'll be friends. But the most beautiful restoration that took place was with the pond.

Our pond had taken years to fill, so we assumed it would take years to refill after being drained. But God had a different plan. Do you remember what He asked me to give my neighbor? One cup of water. Do you know what God gave me back? He brought a rainstorm right over our pond—the heaviest downpour I'd ever seen—and refilled that pond in one day! My friend, those weren't just raindrops that fell that day. To me, it was God lavishing His love all about me and reminding me that He is in absolute control. One cup of water led to the blessing of millions of gallons.

Hosea 10:12 says, "Sow for yourselves righteousness, reap the fruit of unfailing love, and break up your unplowed ground; for it is time to seek the Lord, until He comes and showers righteousness on you."

Now let me have you read that verse again with a few personal additions: "Sow for yourselves righteousness [right choices that honor God even when you don't feel like it], reap the fruit of unfailing love [love for the lovely and unlovely alike], and break up your unplowed ground [whether that be the blockades in your driveway or blockades in your heart]; for it is time to seek the Lord [embrace Him with *all* your heart], until He comes [and He most certainly will] and *showers* [more than you could ever hope for or imagine] righteousness on you."

This is the secret to living the life God has given you and loving it whether you are rejoicing in the sunny good times or feeling tossed and turned in a storm. You have His peace because you have His presence. Give your heart permission to grow in fertile soil by making right choices that honor God every step of the way. Take your eyes off the problem and focus on the good and loving God who has great plans for you. Watch for God to rain down more than you could have ever even thought to ask for. He will restore what has been taken from you in His perfect way. Then you will dance in that rain and drink up every last drop! "The LORD will open the heavens, the storehouse of his bounty, to send rain on your land in season and to bless all the work of your hands" (Deuteronomy 28:12). Are you starting to be amazed by the things that happen when we walk with God?

Personal Bible Study

1. Read Proverbs 25:21-22; Mark 9:41; Hebrews 6:10.

When God asked me to bring my neighbor a cup of water, I was initially resistant to His gentle nudging in my heart. After all, she was persecuting me and putting me and my family through unnecessary turmoil. She did not *deserve* any acts of kindness from me. And then God broke through my selfishness and pointed out that if His judgment was based on what we deserved, I would surely never see heaven. I knew that I needed to stop telling God why my neighbor did not deserve my kindness and simply obey Him. Later, as I reflected on this situation, I thought of these verses, which specifically deal with bringing water in His name. I was encouraged once again by the relevancy of God's living and active Word (Hebrews 4:12) and by His promise that it would not return void (Isaiah 55:10-11). I can rest in that truth, knowing that God has and will use that simple cup of water in my neighbor's life and is now using this story in your life.

2. Read Matthew 25:40; Acts 10:4; Romans 12:13-21.

My assignment was to bring cold water to the person who was trying to block me from entering my home. Your assignment will probably be to bless someone who is just as unworthy in your eyes. Every day, God invites us to reach out in His name to the poor and needy. These people aren't just the financially poor. They are poor in spirit, poor in resources, poor in perspective. They don't just need money or handouts, they need encouragement, kindness, and hope. Many of them don't deserve these things and will probably not appreciate them at first. When I offered that water to my neighbor, she refused it. But God assured me that my willingness to offer it was enough for Him to accomplish His purposes in that time and place. No miracle occurred in that moment; she went on building the fence, and I went home still unaware of exactly how God was going to resolve the situation. But one thing I knew: God was at work, and in that I could rest.

Who is God leading you to reach out to as you read these words? Is there someone in your life who is "the least of these"? Maybe you have an unlovely neighbor as I did. Maybe your "least of these" person is a family member or business associate—or maybe more than one. Pray for God to show you *who* these persons are and what you can do for them in His name—not because they deserve it but because you know that blessing them honors and pleases the Lord. Write down some names and your service in your notebook. Be sure to include the date, and remember to go back later to write what happened as a result. Trust God to multiply your efforts beyond what you can see with your limited vision.

3. Read John 4:4-42.

Though you have probably read this account of the woman at the well before, read it this time paying special attention to Jesus' references to the living water He had to offer her and to what she did after her encounter with Jesus. He so impacted her that she went back and told everyone she could find to tell (verse 28). Verse 39 tells us that "many of the Samaritans from that town believed in Him because of the woman's testimony." Who is God leading you to share your testimony with? Share His living water by telling about your encounters with Him and how He has changed your life.

what gets in my way of knowing god will make a way:
- fear
- negative self-taught
- past experiences
- negative thought from others
*why is so critical not how

Add my name & personalize the scripture
Eph 3:20
Psalm 23
Isaiah 55
Phil 4:19

Eleven

God Will Make a Way

AFTER SUCH AN INCREDIBLE ENDING to the last chapter, you might think that God would send the rain, teach me these great principles, and have the person and me reconcile so we could dance off into the sunset together while "And they lived happily ever after" scrolls across the screen. Well, it was not to be.

About a year after we moved the driveway, a sheriff showed up at our home to serve me papers to appear in court. We were being sued for rent on the time our driveway sat on her property. I almost fainted. Some people have snake phobias, others a fear of heights…not me. I have an overwhelming fear of being taken off to jail. So seeing the sheriff at my door shook me.

Suddenly, my absolute belief that God was in control started to waver. This wavering made me madder than having to go to court. I wanted to believe. I willed myself to stay strong in my belief. I read and reread many "believing" verses like Psalm 118:6-7: "The LORD is with me; I will not be afraid. What can man do to me? The LORD is with me; he is my helper. I will look in triumph on my enemies." Still, I didn't *feel* assured.

I cried out to the Lord. On my more spiritual days my prayers sounded like Psalm 25:1-2: "To you, O LORD, I lift up my soul; in you I trust, O my God…nor let my enemies triumph over me." I knew my "enemy" was not this person—it was Satan wanting me to miserably fail this test. Oh, how I wanted to pass this test, but I was so scared. On my more grumpy, wavering days, I prayed more like Psalm 5:6: "You destroy those who tell lies; bloodthirsty and deceitful men the LORD abhors." Terrible but true.

Treasures to Discover

On and on I vacillated. I was afraid God wouldn't show up for me. What if we lost the court case? How would that make us look? Worse, how would that make God look? The truth all along was that God didn't need me to worry about how He would look or figure out a way to make things turn out okay. God doesn't need us to make excuses for Him when His children simply make the *choice* to believe whether they *feel* assured or not. Our feelings do not have to dictate our choices.

We can choose to believe and walk in that belief with our head held high and our confidence sure. Joyce Meyer agrees:

> I don't always feel like being nice and pleasant, but I can choose to in order to honor God. We live for His glory, not our own pleasure. Dreading things does not glorify God. He wants us to live aggressively, to be alive and face each day with courage. How would any parents feel if their children got up each day and said they feared and dreaded the day their parents had prepared for them? They would, of course, feel terrible. God is a parent—He is our parent.[3]

Psalm 118:24 reminds us, "This is the day the LORD has made; let us rejoice and be glad in it." This day has treasures for us to discover. We will find treasures of truth and treasures of God's presence if we choose to look for them. If we walk through this day with our head downcast, we'll miss the treasures. We'll miss His presence.

We'll miss His assurance. And for sure we'll miss out on rejoicing and being glad in this day.

Through the Blood

If the only things we focus on are the doom and gloom our present circumstances bring us, then we'll wallow in the mud. The mud will cloud our vision, skew our focus, and make us forget that the sun still shines above us. But if we make the choice to rejoice and keep looking up, when we hit the inevitable mud puddle, our shoes might be a little dirty, but it will not affect the way we see life.

The day of our court case I was much calmer than I expected. Though my hands were shaky, my heart was confident. I knew God had gone before us and would work everything out regardless of which way the judge ruled.

Our accuser presented her side of the case, and we presented ours. We were thankful that the judge dismissed the case. At the instant the judge said "dismissed," a beautiful picture popped into my head. One day Jesus will stand between us and our sin, and because of His blood shed on the cross we will hear, "Case dismissed!" What a glorious day that will be!

My heart was rejoicing in this truth as I turned to make my way out of the courtroom. Suddenly, something strange caught my attention and literally took my breath away. It was a trail of blood droplets that led from our courtroom all the way down two halls and out the front doors of the courthouse. (Apparently, some man had a nosebleed. Bless his heart, I feel bad he had to be the one to provide the blood so I could have this wonderful visual!) This man's blood made me think of the blood Jesus shed and of the fact that Jesus' blood leads us out and onward with full assurance. The blood could not be denied that day. It was real. I had to walk through it. Art had to walk through it, and yes, even our accuser had to walk through it. There was no way out except through the blood.

The Pain Has a Purpose

That's when I understood why God allowed this land issue to happen. Romans 8:17 says, "Now if we are children, then we are heirs—heirs of God and co-heirs with Christ, if indeed we share in his sufferings in order that we may also share in his glory." It was a small way to identify and align our hearts with Jesus. And really in the big scheme of things, this was such a little way to suffer. Even if the court ruling had gone the other way, it would have still been such a small way to suffer.

A friend of mine later gave me added perspective. I was telling her about the day the sheriff came to the door and how horrible it was. On and on I went until she asked a simple question: "Lysa, do you know what happened in my life the last time a sheriff knocked on my door?" I didn't know what to say. Her response eliminated my pathetic pity-party: "He was coming to tell me my dad had committed suicide. Do you know how many people are out there today who had a visit from a sheriff? I can almost guarantee you that most of them would trade your visit with theirs in a heartbeat."

How humbling. How true. Yes, we will suffer in this life. Something may be causing you to suffer right now, but the pain has a purpose, and you aren't alone. Jesus is right there with you to comfort you in a way only He can, for He knows what real suffering is like.

We can't even begin to imagine the way Jesus suffered for us. Even our worst sufferings cannot compare to taking the sin of the world upon His body, being nailed to a cross, and dying for people who were beating, spitting on, mocking, and killing Him. Nor can we compare our suffering to God giving His only Son for all this to happen as He, His Father, had to turn and forsake His Son. Yet He did all this so that we can share in His glory. We only have to suffer in comparatively small ways, but we will share in His glory in the grandest of ways.

Renewed Day by Day

Yes indeed, we have no way out except through the blood. This blood-stained path is the way God has made. Through the blood of Jesus we can be saved, we can be healed, we can be taught, and we can be part of an eternal glory that we can't even imagine. Second Corinthians 4:16-17 assures us, "Therefore we do not lose heart. Though outwardly we are wasting away, yet inwardly we are being renewed day by day. For our light and momentary troubles are achieving for us an eternal glory that far outweighs them all."

All parts of that verse are true for me. The eternal glory part is true. The renewed part is true. The troubles part is true. And rest assured, the day-by-day part is so very true. This journey is very day by day for me. Good days, bad days, and all in between days are true for me as well. Some of the comments I receive sound as if people think I lead a very charmed life. Trust me, my life is *so* not charmed. My life is very much like yours.

I get aggravated with those I love the most. I get frustrated with other drivers on the road, especially the ones that beep at me because I drive like Granny Mae. I find myself stepping onto the dreaded scale only to beat myself for not being more self-disciplined. And I'm forever vowing to be more organized, but I keep misplacing the lists my organized friends encourage me to make. No, life is not charmed in the TerKeurst camp any more than it is in your camp.

But I do experience God *in spite* of my circumstances and failures. I see Him. I hear Him. I know He's always close. This is not because I'm special or more spiritual. I experience Him because I choose to. I make choices every day to look for Him, listen for Him, and acknowledge Him. Even though the world tugs at me to serve many lesser gods, in the depths of my heart, I choose Him.

An Open Heart

The decision must be made deep in our heart—not our physical heart but our inner self as a whole. Our thoughts, emotions, intellect, and spirit all combine to form this beautiful spiritual heart within us. The Bible has a lot to say about the heart. It's mentioned more than a thousand times in God's Word. Here are just a few of my favorite verses regarding the heart:

- "Serve the LORD your God with all your heart" (Deuteronomy 10:12).

- "Return to the LORD with all your heart" (1 Samuel 7:3).

- "My heart trusts in him" (Psalm 28:7).

- "So teach *us* to number our days, that we may gain a heart of wisdom" (Psalm 90:12 NKJV).

- "Trust in the LORD with all your heart" (Proverbs 3:5).

- "May he strengthen you with power through his Spirit in your inner being so that Christ may dwell in your hearts" (Ephesians 3:16-17).

To make the decision to experience God, you must have a heart that's open to Him. When we forget to be renewed day by day by looking and listening for God, we lose our eternal perspective, get entangled in the troubles of today, and close our heart to Him.

A closed heart simply and tragically forgets God.

Though I may fall short in many areas of my life, I will not close my heart to God. I will rejoice in really believing Him. The purpose of this phase will then be fulfilled when I know He is too real to deny. In every circumstance I face, I know God makes a way, not because life is always hunky-dory but because I've chosen to experience Him too many times to live any other way. May it be so with you as well.

Personal Bible Study

1. Read Isaiah 29:13; Matthew 15:8.

These two passages talk about following a religion based on rules and regulations without committing our hearts to Him. Honoring God with our lips by merely talking about Christianity is one thing. Honoring Him with our hearts by entering into a relationship with Him is another thing entirely.

2. Read 1 Samuel 3:20.

God promises that if we honor Him, He will honor us. We can honor the Lord in many ways. I have listed below some key ways to honor God. Read each verse for yourself and write down specific ways you can apply it to your life as you honor God.

- Psalm 50:23—We can honor Him with our thankfulness.
- Ephesians 5:21-33—We can honor Him as His bride by giving ourselves up for Him and respecting Him.
- Psalm 91:15—We can honor Him by calling on Him, making communication part of our daily relationship with Him.
- John 14:23-24—We can honor Him by obeying His teachings.

Proverbs 8:17 says, "I love those who love me, and those who seek me find me." Seek God with all of your heart, and don't be satisfied with merely paying lip service to having a relationship with Him.

2. Read Luke 11:28; John 13:17; James 1:22-25.

These passages highlight three key elements: hearing the Word of God, doing what it says, and receiving a blessing as a result. Isn't it interesting how this chain of events works? These passages describe hearing the Word by taking it in, allowing it to work within you, and then using what you have learned to benefit others and to further God's kingdom. Jesus came to serve us as a living example that we are to follow in our lives. As we serve those around us—our husband, children, parents, or even those we consider to be unlovely—Jesus has blessings in store for us. Just as we cannot merely follow a religion without a relationship, neither can we merely hear the Word without acting on it. Do not allow yourself to have eyes that do not see and ears that do not hear. Do not go through life with a closed heart. Take steps today to live out your faith in a way that impacts those around you. Write down one way that God is leading you to become a doer of the Word. Prayerfully commit before the Lord to take this step today.

3. Read Hebrews 13:20-21.

I shared in this chapter about the blood we had to walk through as we left the courthouse and the powerful visual reminder that was for me. This verse tells us that through Jesus' atoning blood, we are equipped with everything we need to do His will. Through Jesus, God has fully provided everything we need and made us ready to actively live out our faith according to His plans and His purposes for us. We don't need to worry about our abilities or our shortcomings when we know we already have all we need through Jesus. What inadequacies inhibit you from stepping out and acting on your faith? List them in your notebook, and as you draw a line through each one, thank God today for covering all of them through Jesus Christ, to whom be the glory for ever and ever. Amen.

Twelve

Learning to Lead

GOD IS CALLING YOU TO LIVE OUT His dream for you, and part of the dream is to lead. As we seek to believe God like never before, we will set an example for others to follow. I never pictured myself as a leader until God revealed to me that like it or not, people were watching and modeling my life. If you are influencing people, you are a leader. You may not stand before crowds or be the next Kay Arthur, but in some way, God will use you to lead others through your influence in their life. Do you not only believe God but also believe in God's calling on your life?

Maybe your reaction to this revelation is like Moses' three-part response.

1. I'm not _____ enough!

"Who am I that I should go to Pharaoh, and that I should bring the children of Israel out of Egypt?" (Exodus 3:11).

In so many words, we tell God, I'm not qualified. I'm not educated enough. I'm not old enough. I'm too old. I'm not wealthy enough. I'm not smart enough. I'm not brave enough. I'm not bold enough. I'm not organized enough. And on and on and on we go with excuses.

2. What if others reject me?

"But suppose they will not believe me or listen to my voice; suppose they say, 'The LORD has not appeared to you?'" (Exodus 4:1).

Who are we more concerned about pleasing: other people or God? We are not responsible to control how others act and react. We are simply responsible to do what God tells us to do. Certainly, we should listen to wise, godly counsel. But laying our agendas and desires aside, we must first go to God in His Word and in prayer, spending time listening to Him.

3. What if I mess up?

"O my Lord, I *am* not eloquent, neither before or since You have spoken to Your servant; but I *am* slow of speech and slow of tongue" (Exodus 4:10 NKJV).

As we've seen already, one thing was true about each of the heroes of the Bible—they each messed up. But they chose not to wallow in the mud of their mistakes. Instead, they kept a responsive heart toward God. We need to be like David, who is the only one God ever called a man after His own heart. When he messed up, he cried out, "Create in me a pure heart, O God, and renew a steadfast spirit within me. Do not cast me from your presence or take your holy spirit from me. Restore to me the joy of your salvation and grant me a willing spirit, to sustain me. Then I will teach transgressors your ways, and sinners will turn back to you" (Psalm 51:10-13).

God will reveal to us not only when we mess up but how to return to Him if we constantly seek a pure heart. Is it easy? No, it's extremely difficult to come face-to-face with our sin and admit our failures. That's why David had to ask for a "willing spirit." But did you catch the beautiful outcome? God will redeem our failures! God will take our mess-ups, what Satan meant for our defeat, and use the situation for His glory. People stuck in the same sin you're in will find their way back to God by hearing your story.

God Uses Inadequate People

The truth is that God has already given you a place of influence, and you are the right person for the job. God calls inadequate people so He can work through them and He can receive the glory that is only His. When you experience God working through you despite your human shortcomings, your confidence in Him and His abilities will grow more than ever before. God rarely uses people who look perfect. He uses *imperfect* people.

You know the "perfect people" I'm talking about. We've all had people in our lives who think they are experts on every topic that comes up. Maybe we've even acted this way at times. The Bible calls this being "stiff-necked," which is a picture of being deceived and hardened. Second Chronicles 30:8 says, "Do not be stiff-necked, as your fathers were; submit to the LORD."

Think about this picture. A stiff-necked person has one of two problems. Either she refuses to turn her head or she refuses to bow her head. If we are too proud and think we know it all, we are stiff-necked because we refuse to bow our head and admit our inadequacies. If we are too insecure, we are stiff-necked because we refuse to look at the possibilities that God is placing around us. The cure for either is submission to God—which means yielding our thoughts, emotions, fears, and wills to Him.

The Cure for a Stiff Neck

Moses overcame his stiff-necked attitude and inadequate feelings by walking in obedience with God. Step-by-step, he started obeying God and eventually became the leader God knew he could be. In Deuteronomy 10:12-16, Moses gives the children of Israel a description of what God expects from us.

> And now, O Israel, what does the LORD your God ask of
> you but to fear the LORD your God, to walk in all His

ways, to love him, to serve the LORD your God with all your heart and with all your soul, and to observe the LORD's commands and decrees that I am giving you today for your own good? To the LORD your God belongs the heavens, even the highest heavens, the earth and everything in it. Yet the LORD set his affection on your forefathers and loved them, and he chose you, their descendants, above all the nations, as it is today. Circumcise your hearts, therefore, and do not be stiffnecked any longer.

Actually, we all have stiff-necked tendencies. Before we can overcome them, we must have our hearts circumcised. The males of Egypt were required to be circumcised surgically. Moses learned the extreme importance of this when he almost lost his life due to not having his own son circumcised in a timely manner. God could not have Moses be the deliverer of His people until the requirement of circumcision had been fulfilled. And the same is true of our hearts being circumcised as well. The physical act of circumcision gives us a visual of this spiritual truth. The commentary in the NIV Life Application Study Bible includes this note:

But God wanted them to go beyond the surgery to understanding its meaning. They needed to submit to God on the inside, in their hearts, as well as outside, in their bodies. Then they could begin to imitate God's love and justice in their relationships with others. If our hearts are right, then our relationships with other people can be made right too. When your heart has been cleansed and you have been reconciled with God, you will begin to see a difference in the way you treat others.[4]

Actions and Reactions

So to be the leader God wants you to be, you have to not only believe in God's calling on your life but also believe that the people you are leading are valuable and worthy to be honored. Moses learned to be a *good* leader by walking in obedience to God. Moses developed into a *great* leader by being consistent enough with his habits of obedience that they became the natural reactions of his heart. The way to be a *good* leader is for your *actions* to be reflective of God reigning inside you. But to be a *great* leader is for your *reactions* to be reflective of God reigning inside you. Did you catch that? Your reactions are key.

We can easily choose to act obediently to the Lord and honor others in times of less stress. I can be the best mother in the world sitting quietly at the library reading parenting books while my kids are at home with a sitter. The real test is when I go home and something happens to turn the stress up a few notches. How will I react? That reaction is the real litmus test revealing the condition of my heart. My reactions let me know whether or not my belief in God and His ability to shape and mold me is real. Remember, the purpose of this believing phase is to get you to the place where your experience of God is too real to deny.

Nothing will make God so real to you as seeing Him change your character. Not change *who* you are—your personality, your strengths, and your abilities—but *how* you are—your character. I like what the Life Application Study Bible says in its commentary on Moses:

> In Moses we see an outstanding personality shaped by God. But we must not misunderstand what God did. He did not change who or what Moses was; he did not give Moses new abilities and strengths. Instead, he took Moses' characteristics and molded them until they were suited to his purposes. Does knowing this make a difference in your understanding of God's purpose in your life? He is trying to take what he created in the first place and use it for his intended purposes.[5]

Moses and the Phases of Faith

Moses struggled with both his actions and his reactions. God taught Moses to obey by letting him live with the consequences of his disobedience. His time in the desert after murdering an abusive Egyptian proved to be invaluable. He had to leave the comforts of the palace he'd grown up in (phase one) and endure a famine-like experience of becoming a lowly shepherd (phase two) to get to the place where he could learn to really believe (phase three). This is another example of God taking a bad situation and using it for good. Living in the desert, herding a flock, and learning to hear from God prepared Moses for the role he was destined to play. And it prepared him to move through the next two phases of death and resurrection.

Those are some of the many experiences God used to make Moses into the man that Hebrews 11:24-27 describes:

> By faith Moses, when he had grown up, refused to be known as the son of Pharaoh's daughter. He chose to be mistreated along with the people of God rather than to enjoy the pleasures of sin for a short time. He regarded disgrace for the sake of Christ as of greater value than the treasures of Egypt, because he was looking ahead to his reward. By faith he left Egypt, not fearing the king's anger; he persevered because he saw him who is invisible.

Oh to have such things said about me when I'm gone!

Believing or Grumbling?

When I consider all the lessons Moses had to learn, the one experience that I learn the most from is the one that prevented Moses from entering the earthly promised land. This scene breaks my heart, but it's worth studying because of the rich spiritual truths it demonstrates. The children of Israel left Egypt 40 years earlier. Most of the original people had died, and only their children and grandchildren remained. Moses, Aaron, Joshua, and Caleb were among the remaining few. Sadly, the children of Israel were singing the same grumbling song: "Why did you bring the LORD's community into this desert, that we and our livestock should die here? Why did you bring us up out of Egypt to this terrible place? It has no grain or figs, grapevines or pomegranates. And there is no water to drink!" (Numbers 20:4-5).

Most of these Israelites had never personally tasted a fig, grape, or pomegranate. They only knew desert life. All they knew about what they were missing was what they learned from their disobedient and grumbling parents. These parents had many stories they could have shared to constantly remind their children of God's faithfulness. Instead, negative attitudes consumed their hearts. So, tragically, this is what they passed to their children. This is probably what grieved Moses the most as he threw himself facedown before the Lord and asked what to do.

Moses' Disobedience

"The LORD said to Moses, 'Take your staff, and you and your brother Aaron gather the assembly together. Speak to the rock before their eyes and it will pour out its water'" (Numbers 20:7-8).

In Exodus 17, God had instructed Moses to strike a rock, and water came out. But this time Moses was to only speak to the rock. God was teaching the people to do what He says, though it makes no sense, and watch Him keep His promises. In Joshua 6, the walls of Jericho fall by the shouts of the people. Therefore, Numbers 20 records a pivotal moment that could have proved to the people that God can use voices—He can bring water from a rock or, as they would later see, tear down walls. But Moses, in his frustration and bad reaction to the people's grumbling, did not obey the Lord. Instead of speaking to the rock, he struck it twice.

The water came, but so did God's harsh punishment for Moses.

"But the LORD said to Moses and Aaron, 'Because you did not trust in me enough to honor me as holy in the sight of the Israelites, you will not bring this community into the land I give them'" (Numbers 20:12).

We might expect this point of the story to be filled with great weeping and gnashing of teeth. But we have no record of any kind of negative reaction. No begging for mercy, no cry for a "do-over," no pleading for an exception, no long "that's not fair" speech... nothing. Moses' reaction appears to finally have been shaped and molded to reflect God's reign in him.

Moses and the Promise

Moses never physically entered the promised land, but two additional points are worth noting. First, Moses desired God's presence more than he desired to enter the promised land. In Exodus 33:18-23, Moses' secret desire to see God comes to pass. Though he only got to see His back, he saw God nonetheless. Once he saw God, everything else paled in comparison. Maybe this is why being excluded from the promised land didn't appear to rattle him. He remained focused and continued leading the people. My flesh would have been tempted to leave those whiny Israelites to fend for themselves in the desert while I went off and pouted the rest of my dying days under a rock somewhere. But Moses didn't react in his flesh. He remained faithful and true. He unselfishly finished his mission. Hebrews 11 remembers him as one who "persevered because he saw him who is invisible."

Secondly, many years after Moses' death, he appears with Jesus on the Mount of Transfiguration, which just happens to be in the physical location of the promised land. "Just then there appeared before them Moses and Elijah, talking with Jesus" (Matthew 17:3). Did you catch that? Moses was standing in the promised land, talking with Jesus. When he desired to see God before, he could only see His back, but now he sees Him face-to-face. How precious of God to give us this beautiful reminder that He always comes through for us. He wants our dreams to come true more than we do. He has everything planned out, and even if things don't seem to work out on this side of glory, we can't even imagine how amazing eternity will be. "No eye has seen, no ear has heard, no mind has conceived what God has prepared for those who love him" (1 Corinthians 2:9).

My friend, I pray that along this journey of walking with God toward your dream, your greatest joy will be seeing and experiencing God, for that is the real joy of this entire adventure!

Personal Bible Study

1. Read Exodus 2:1-10; Acts 7:20-22; Hebrews 11:23.

God, Moses' parents, and Pharaoh's daughter all saw that Moses was no ordinary child. Indeed, he was the chosen deliverer God raised up as the leader of all Israel. Though Pharaoh's daughter didn't know it at the time, she was participating in God's plan for one special child. Only God could arrange for Moses to live in the palace of the very man who was trying to kill him! Because of his upbringing in the palace, Moses had the finest education and resources of the day. He understood Egyptian culture from the inside, which gave him a perspective unlike any other Israelite of his time. The only thing Moses lacked from his Egyptian upbringing was a close walk with God. Moses' 40 years in the desert gave God ample time to remedy that situation.

As Moses served as a shepherd and lived as an outcast from his people, God worked in his heart. God used Moses' time in the desert to work on his character, making his preparation complete. In the desert, God revealed His plan for Moses. God's plan for each one of us includes a unique preparation for our particular assignment. What has God prepared you for? What is He preparing you for now? Is God speaking to you in a desert time? Is He preparing your heart for something big enough to take your breath away? God gave us Moses' example to assure us that He is working a plan for our lives even when we cannot see it. Moses became a man of influence because God prepared in advance for Him to be one. In your notebook, write down some of the truths you have learned from your desert times. How is God using those truths to prepare you?

2. Read Exodus 4:10-17; Ecclesiastes 4:10; Mark 6:7.

When Moses offered up excuse after excuse to God, God responded by providing him with Aaron, his brother, to speak for him. God recognized Moses' need for a partner who would encourage and support him in his calling. We also read that Jesus sent His disciples out "two by two." Clearly, God understands we need people in our lives to stand by us and cheer us on in our calling. Has God provided you with a friend, spouse, or relative who encourages you in your walk and prays for you? Thank God for that person today. If that is something you lack, you can ask God to provide such a person for you. Above all else, remember that God has already given you "a friend that sticks closer than a brother" (Proverbs 18:24). Spend some time today thanking God for being your Friend.

3. Read Exodus 4:19-20; Jeremiah 10:23.

Once Moses fully trusted God and overcame his fears, he returned to Egypt. God assured him that he would be safe in his travels, and Moses set out on his faith journey step-by-step. Sometimes our steps feel like baby steps, and we wonder if we are getting anywhere. All God asks is that we take steps of obedience and let Him take care of the rest. What step is God asking you to take? Don't worry about where the journey will take you. Trust God with the journey as you take each step. You take care of the possible and let Him take care of the impossible.

PHASE FOUR

Death

Thirteen

Death Does Not
Mean Defeat

THE THIRD PHASE OF THE WALK OF FAITH, the beautiful time of believing God like never before, is a wonderful time that we might hope will continue forever. But God has more to teach us, and we must be willing to enter into yet another season of growth. Surprisingly, the fourth phase is called Death. But don't let the name discourage you. Death brings about a new life that can't be found any other way. Indeed, death does not mean defeat.

I went to college to get an education, but that's not all I wanted. The degree I really wanted was not a bachelor's or even a master's but a Mrs. I had it all planned out, really. I would find Mr. Wonderful, we'd fall in love, date throughout college, become engaged my senior year, and get married the weekend after graduation. So, right from the first day on campus I scanned every crowd looking for *him*. I was subtle about it and played hard to get, but I mentally cross-examined every guy I met to discern if he could be the one.

I didn't discover *him* until my sophomore year. But the minute I first laid eyes on him, I was captured. He was tall, dark, handsome, and the star of the football team. He was on billboards throughout the town and posters all over campus. And he was supersmart. Majoring in physics, he maintained a 4.0 GPA. Though I had never graced the halls of the science building, I signed up for Physics 101. Then, I proceeded to fail my first test and suddenly was in desperate need of a tutor. What a beautiful plan to get to meet with *him* on a regular basis!

To protect the innocent we'll call him Flicktoid, or Flick for short. Before long, our tutoring became less and less about physics and more about the chemistry budding between us. I dropped the class, but the relationship was in full bloom and continued long after physics was forgotten.

The Big Surprise

We dated all throughout the rest of our college career. I filled pages of scrapbooks that would one day be a treasure to show our children. I imagined the faces of mini-me's and mini-he's all gathering around our kitchen table, gazing in delight as I recounted our romance. *Here's a petal from the first roses Daddy gave me. Oh, and here's a picture from a formal dance we went to in the mountains. And look, Daddy's football team won the national championship that year. What a star he was. There's Mommy cheering him on from the stands. I went to every game.*

Flick graduated a year before me and went on to a graduate school that was four hours away. We continued dating, and as my graduation approached, my anticipation grew. We had talked about getting engaged, and I thought the big question could come anytime. Each time we saw each other, I imagined this could be the big day. But graduation came and went, and still no ring.

When I was deciding on where to move after graduation, he encouraged me to get a job close to his school. I was able to move only a few hours from him, and I was sure this was a good sign. Though I was lonely in this new town, I was encouraged by the fact that my birthday was only a few weeks away. I decided this must be what he was waiting on and swept away any doubts as to the future.

Flick arrived late for our date on my birthday, complaining about the drive being too far for just a dinner date. As the evening wore on, other clues should have warned me that things weren't going as I'd hoped. But my Pollyanna attitude just kept me wishing for the best. At the end of dinner, Flick pushed back his chair, took my hand, and looked me straight in the eyes. Oh, finally, the big moment!

It was big all right. Flick announced he'd met someone else. I had hardly picked my jaw up off the floor when he continued, "And I really need to be getting back. Do you have a few bucks I can borrow for gas?" I was in such shock that I not only paid for my own birthday dinner but also for his gas to get back to the new Flickette!

The Pit

The story sounds funny now, but at the time it seemed worse than death. I was so alone. I had uprooted my whole life and planned my future around him. Now he was gone, and so were all my grand dreams to get married. I was angry, hurt, depressed, and devastated. The rejection from this man I trusted stung deeply. It sent me into a dark pit of depression. I couldn't eat, couldn't sleep, and couldn't fathom how I'd ever get over this hurt.

I crawled into bed, pulled the covers over my head, and didn't care if I ever saw the light of day again. Though my responsibilities eventually made me get out of bed, I just went through the motions of living. Inside my heart, I was under that blanket of darkness.

One Saturday morning, my roommate bounded into my room, holding up a newspaper ad for a large church near our apartment. Though she was not a churchgoer herself, she encouraged me to go and meet some people my age. She quipped, "That church is so big, you might even find your husband!"

So I went to that big church the next day. Though I found no husband right away, I did find some great friends who helped me get over Flick. More importantly, I shifted my opinions about what really mattered in a husband. Almost a year later, one of my guy friends from my Bible study group introduced me to the most handsome man I'd ever met…handsome on the outside, and even more importantly, handsome on the inside as well. We became friends, but I secretly hoped for more.

Nothing but the Best

About this time—you guessed it—Flick started calling again. Things hadn't worked out with Flickette, and he claimed to now see the error in his ways. He wanted me back. He wanted us to be together again, forever. Even though I didn't know if the new young man I had taken an interest in would ever ask me out, I knew I was at a major crossroads. Flick was everything I thought I wanted. A year earlier, I would have given anything to have him back—but not now. I had a new vision for what love was supposed to be. My new interest treated me nicely, encouraged me in my relationship with the Lord, and bought my dinner when a group of us went out—and we weren't even dating!

I called Flick and told him it was over for good. Nothing he could do or say would change that. Though there were no assurances that anything would ever work out with the young man from church, I was assured that God didn't want me to settle for anything less than His best.

A few weeks later, the young man from church finally asked me out. His name was Art TerKeurst…and eight months later, we were married. Now, I must say, our marriage has not always been easy. I now know that all those years of so desperately wanting someone to love me were not cries for a husband but rather for a Savior. My soul yearned for a relationship with the Lord though my heart had been fooled into thinking all my wrongs would be fixed with a husband. But Art has weathered my emotional and spiritual storms in a way that Flick never would have.

God's Way Might Not Be the Shortest Way

Art is the perfect husband for me. God knew what I needed so much better than I did. Thank God for not answering the prayers for Flick and me to get married. Flick breaking my heart was one of the best things that ever happened to me. It was a death of sorts but not a defeat. It was a victory in disguise.

So much about my life has been like that. The very things that feel like death are really a birth of something so much better. Later in this section we'll learn a lot about the children of Israel and their journey to the promised land. But first I want to recap their initial day of deliverance. It wasn't the day they left Egypt; it was the day God radically delivered them from the pursuit of their captors.

The children of Israel were led by God, not on the shortest route but rather the *ordained* route. Exodus 13:21 says, "By day the LORD went ahead of them in a pillar of cloud to guide them on their way and by night in a pillar of fire to give them light, so they could travel by day or night." God was with them and reassured them of His presence in visible ways. But they reached a point in their exodus from Egypt when, though they knew God was there, they felt defeated. Just when they thought they'd escaped the Egyptians, Pharaoh's army appeared on the horizon, barreling toward them. "They were terrified and cried out to the LORD... 'It would have been better to serve the Egyptians than to die in the desert!'" (Exodus 14:10-12).

His Way Is Perfect

Oh, how I can relate to their anguish and utter dismay. I too was in a strange place when Flick broke up with me. I couldn't understand why God had brought me to this place only to allow my heart to get broken. But if I'd never moved to be closer to Flick, I would have never met Art. It wasn't the shortest route or even the safest in my opinion, but it was God's best, and I'm so thankful I stuck with

Him. Left to my own opinions and plans, who knows where I'd be today.

Just as God didn't abandon me, He didn't abandon the Israelites either. "Moses answered the people, 'Do not be afraid. Stand firm and you will see the deliverance the LORD will bring you today. The Egyptians you see today you will never see again. The LORD will fight for you; you only need to be still'" (Exodus 14:13-14).

The minute they stopped fretting, the Lord started fighting. He told the Israelites to move on through the sea. Moses raised his hand over the sea, and the water parted, allowing the Israelites a way of escape. With a wall of water to their right and left, the Israelites crossed over on dry land. When Pharaoh followed them, the Lord caused the sea to crash back on top of them, and the Egyptian army perished that day.

The sea in front of them must have looked so big, so dangerous, so immovable. The army behind them was deadly, horrifying, and so seemingly unstoppable. But the Lord was bigger than the immovable and stronger than the unstoppable. Israel had no way to escape, but God cut a new path and made a way. Not only did He make a way but He defeated the Egyptians, so as God had promised, Israel never saw those Egyptians again. His strength was perfect. His timing was perfect. His plan was perfect.

Death Is Defeated

And so it is with our lives as well. Death seems frightening, but it is not to be feared. As you walk through death times in your journey of faith, rest assured that God has already defeated death. "Since the children have flesh and blood, he too shared in their humanity so that by his death he might destroy him who holds the power of death—that is, the devil—and free those who all their lives were held in slavery by their fear of death" (Hebrews 2:14-15).

God not only has defeated death but is providing victory through it. This is not your defeat; this is your valley in the shadow of the mountain your soul longs to climb—a mountain of greater faith and closer intimacy with God than you ever thought possible.

> I have set the LORD always before me. Because he is at my right hand, I will not be shaken. Therefore my heart is glad and my tongue rejoices; my body also will rest secure, because you will not abandon me to the grave, nor will you let your Holy One see decay. You have made known to me the path of life; you will fill me with joy in your presence, with eternal pleasures at your right hand (Psalm 16:8-11).

When you die, your body will go to the grave, but you can rest assured that with God your soul will never taste defeat.

Personal Bible Study

1. Read Jeremiah 23:23-24.

God is not a distant God, seated on a throne far away. He is a living, active God—aware of every thought, every need, every heartbreak, every death in our lives. We need only to call out to Him, and He will invade our dark secret places full of shame and tears and shine His light in our hearts. Little by little we can know His love and let His hope replace our sorrow so we can look ahead with our trust firmly rooted in Him. In your notebook, write a short prayer asking God to be very real to you.

2. Read Psalm 139:1-10.

Some days I do this thing called life really well. That's when I feel like verse 8: "If I go up to the heavens, you are there." On those days, I am communing with God, and His praise is on my lips. Then there are those days when I really stink at life. I feel cut off from God as though my prayers hit the ceiling and bounce back down into my lap. David finishes verse 8 with this: "If I make my bed in the depths, you are there." God is with us on our "praising Jesus" days and in our "want to curl up in bed with the covers over our head" days. He is still there on our bad days, singing over us (Zephaniah 3:17), wiping our tears (Isaiah 25:8), and taking care of our future (Jeremiah 29:11).

When I lost my college love, I thought my life was over. I "made my bed in the depths" for a while as I grieved this loss. I could not see that what I thought was an ending was only the beginning. God was working out His plans for me—I just had to trust Him. Do you need to trust God with something?

3. Maybe God seems very far away right now. Don't believe that lie. He is a very involved Father, as the Scriptures show us. Write

out these verses in your notebook and note how God is personally ministering to you through each: Isaiah 25:8; Jeremiah 29:11; Zephaniah 3:17.

4. Read Habakkuk 1:5; Acts 13:26-41.

What is the "something" Habakkuk says the Jews would not believe? Acts applies this verse to Christ's death, burial, and resurrection—which came to pass exactly as the prophets foretold. I like the verse in Habakkuk and can tell you of many times when God has made things happen in my life that I could not believe. From meeting my handsome, gift-of-God husband to speaking and writing books like this, I stand amazed at what God has done, just as the verse says. I thank God for His plan for my life, and I have learned to trust Him each day.

Think back on your life for a moment. Try to recall a time when you can definitely see God at work in your life even though at the time you wondered if He had forgotten you. Death did not mean defeat then, and it doesn't now. Write about this time in your notebook and pray about sharing your story. If you are not going through this book with a group, pray about sharing your story with a friend.

5. You might want to pray Ephesians 3:20-21 when you are finished with this portion of the Bible study. Spend some time really praising God for how He has brought about victories in your life. Praise Him that the power that resurrected Jesus is at work in our lives today! Write some of your praises in your notebook.

Fourteen

Pressing Through the Pain

MARY WAS AN AMAZING WOMAN. Every person she touched was changed for good. In big ways and small ways, Mary was a woman of grace, love, and sweet influence. Being invited to one of Mary's parties was always the highlight of any holiday. Her goal was to let her gift of hospitality shine for God's glory, and shine it did. Though she always wowed attendees, her goal wasn't to impress people but rather to love them. Whether at a simple family gathering or a grand gala with many, she always made each person feel special and important.

So you can imagine how loved Mary's husband always felt. They had been married since Mary was 20 years and two weeks old, and they were madly in love even after 40 years of marriage. Ken and Mary moved down the street from me several years ago and always inspired me with their love, devotion, and life full of fun. Their sunny yellow house was as happy on the inside as it always looked on the outside.

When Mary found out she had cancer, she handled the news with the same cheerful poise and positive attitude that she'd handled all of life. She and Ken battled the disease together and were two of the bravest fighters I've ever witnessed. He was always at her side. She was always smiling.

Everyone thought Mary would beat the cancer and come out skipping on the other side, but it was not to be. They traveled to Houston to participate in a very aggressive treatment program and kept up with family and friends through website postings.

I couldn't read these postings in Mary's last days without sobbing. When she finally went to be with the Lord, I felt as if the whole world paused for a minute of sadness as this ray of sunshine left this place. And there was Ken, alone. The hand he'd held for most of his life was now still. The smile he'd found such joy in seeing was now gone. The voice he'd delighted in hearing was now silent. How do you press through such pain?

Enjoy Life

A few weeks after the celebration of Mary's life, I ran into Ken when my kids and I were out eating lunch. He was alone. I asked how he was doing, and though he smiled, his response broke my heart.

"The silence is killing me," he admitted.

Without pausing, I insisted he come to our house for dinner. I gave the disclaimer that I'm not the best cook, I couldn't guarantee what the house might look like, and we are quite a lively bunch but I could guarantee there would be no silence. He accepted.

When Ken arrived, life was very hectic at my house. The boys were picking on their sisters, the puppy wet the carpet again, the phone was ringing, my youngest was jumping on the couch, and I was trying to manage the two pots and a casserole dish that contained our dinner. I apologized for not remembering to offer him something to drink right away. When he graciously said, "No problem," he added, "Enjoy this, Lysa. Enjoy every moment. It goes by so fast."

Throughout the evening, Ken continued with this same gentle reminder. Though he said it in different ways and at different times, the message was always the same. *Savor every moment of this precious time. Life is here. Precious, loud, hectic, messy, beautiful, rich, irreplaceable life is here. And the time to enjoy life like this is short.*

Look for His Answers

We had a delightful evening with Ken. We'd invited him to dinner as a gift, but we were the ones who received the real treasure. As he was leaving and Art was walking him to his car, he stopped halfway down the sidewalk. He walked over to a gardenia bush planted in front of our house—a bush I've breezed by without enjoying for eleven years. He bent down to a flower on one of the lower branches and buried his face in it while breathing in deeply.

The sight made my breath catch in my throat. I knew Ken had been crying out to the Lord to fill in the gaps Mary left—her gentleness, her sweet smell, her beauty, and her way of brightening up any place she went. Ken prayed expectantly. He expected God to answer and therefore was able to recognize the answer when it came. A flower handcrafted by the hand of God was designed, I'm convinced, just for Ken.

That's the secret of pressing through the pain. Really, it's the secret of pressing through all of life. Learning to depend on God, asking for His provision, and then remembering to look for His ready answers. God did more that night than remind Ken of His faithfulness. He reminded me of what is really important and how to press through the pain with perspective.

As a woman, perspective sometimes gets lost in the sea of emotions that course through my heart. A woman's heart is a deep, wild, and wondrous place full of secret desires. I desire for my life to count for something. I desire for my kids to grow and become good people. I desire for my marriage to always be full of love and devotion. I desire to live a life of no regrets. But my greatest secret desire must always be for more of God in my life. This is the only desire that's certain to never disappoint and can never be taken from me. My husband, my kids, and my life as I know it could be stripped away in an instant. But God will be there through it all. I just have to make the choice to make my relationship with Him of utmost importance.

Knowing this for sure, I can press through any and every pain, disappointment, and even death. God is near. He's drawing me close, teaching me lessons I can't learn any other way, revealing more of His character, allowing me to experience Him in even more amazing ways. Yes, death is hard and extremely painful. Whether it's a loved one, a lifestyle, or a dream, death hurts. I know—I've passed through this phase many times in many different ways. But rather than only looking at what the death phase takes, I've learned to see the good it gives.

God's Presence in Little Things

Sometimes when we go through the death phase of our faith walk, we get so consumed with trying to find the big resurrection that we forget to see God reveal Himself in smaller ways throughout our day.

I asked a friend who is going through a very hard death phase to write down every little thing the Lord had done the previous day to remind her of His love. She was amazed how much more clearly she could see God's hand as she retraced her steps and stopped to ponder this. She'd gotten lost traveling home from visiting family and cried out to God how unfair it was that she was lost. But her circuitous route took her by her favorite restaurant, where she was able to enjoy the very thing she wanted for lunch and still make it home on time. On the same trip, at one point her cruise control stopped working. She slowed down to adjust the knobs to try and fix it. Only then did she realize the speed limit had decreased and a police officer was behind her. Had her cruise control not malfunctioned at that moment, she probably would have kept going the same speed and gotten a ticket.

My friend sensed God's presence in her favorite lunch and no speeding ticket. Ken saw His handiwork in a beautiful flower. How has God revealed His presence to you today? If your desire is for more of Him, you can rest assured that He is working to show you something wonderful right now.

Personal Bible Study

1. Read Exodus 15:1-21.

As the children of Israel crossed the Red Sea and emerged on the other side, they stopped and sang praises to the Lord. As we see God at work in our lives, do we stop and praise Him? Do we pause in the midst of our busy lives to deeply inhale the beauty of His creation? Do we choose to focus on the special moments He has given to us and treasure them as a praise song in our hearts to Him? Record your thoughts in your notebook.

2. Read Psalm 22:3-5; 99:1-3.

These verses tell us that God—who is holy and majestic beyond our comprehension—inhabits our praises. If we want to experience a closer walk with Him, we need only to praise Him. His presence will overwhelm us when we choose to get off the normal path and notice the blessings He sends our way each day. May we learn to send up prayers of thanks and praise as we go through our days.

We can pray prayers of thanksgiving for what He does for us: *Thank You, Father, for the sound of laughter. Thank You, Father, for the beautiful weather. Thank You, Father, for knowing what is best for me. Thank You, Father, for Your plan for my life.* Record some things you are thankful for.

We can also praise Him simply for who He is. *I praise You, Father, for Your sovereignty. I praise You, Lord, for being Lord of all. You, O Lord, are my King, my Rock, my Redeemer. I praise You and You alone.* This song can be always on our lips as we commune with Him in the midst of our days. Record some praises for who God is to you personally.

Do the same thing I asked my friend to do: Think back to yesterday and write down every little way God assured you that He was with you.

3. Read 2 Corinthians 10:5.

Underline the phrase "take captive every thought." God is a God of details. He is orderly. He is in control. He is intentional about everything He does. And so He desires us to be intentional too. Just as we should take captive every thought, so we should take captive every moment to praise Him. Are you letting these moments pass you by? What is distracting you from praising God more often, and how can you make praising him more often a priority?

4. I walked down my sidewalk for 11 years, never diverging from my routine to stop and take captive a moment to rejoice in a gift God had waiting for me if I only looked. Ken's lesson to me that night was to take captive every moment to notice the blessings in my life, both big and small, and to give God the praise when I do.

Write down a praise to the Lord in your notebook. Specifically praise Him for a way He provided for you recently. Your provision may have come in an unexpected way but was no less an answer to your prayers. Ken prayed for more time with his beloved Mary. Instead he is learning to see God's provision in other ways on earth until the day he will join Mary to praise Him in heaven. God will meet all of our needs just as He has met Ken's. Take captive every moment to focus on His gifts to you, regardless of your circumstances. Write your praise for His provision for you in your notebook.

Fifteen

God Isn't Surprised by Death

Have you ever noticed that nature doesn't resist God? Think of the little seed that is planted. It's pushed down into a place that's dark and messy. Then it must go through a death of sorts. The seed must cease to exist as a seed as its shell starts to disintegrate and crack open before life can spring from it. When it follows God's design, life springs from the seed, pushes through the dirt, and finds life in the light. Who would have thought that a glorious plant could come from a tiny seed in a dark place?

What would have happened had the seed resisted God and retained its original shape? It would have avoided the trauma of change, but think of all it would have missed out on. It would never have known God's best. How we are so like that little seed at times!

The Seed of a Vision

I have acted like that seed and resisted God when the task placed before me seemed too big, too time consuming, too risky, too costly. I acted like that seed when God gave me the vision for my personal ministry assignment. *How, God?* I felt so small, so unable, so afraid of trying and failing. As my ministry began, I was willing to take on the small tasks God gave me. I did so for many years, reaching many women with a message of encouragement. But I knew God wanted me to take a new step. *How, God?*

Then the thought struck me that maybe I could speak at an arena event along with other speakers.

The other, more famous speakers could draw the crowd, I could fulfill my own assignment, and we'd all sing Kum-ba-yah and go home happy. So I started praying for an arena event. Don't you just love it when people try to make suggestions to God? (Ugh…note to self: this is *not* a good idea.)

I was thrilled when I finally received the invitation. I was invited to speak at an arena event with an expected attendance of five thousand people. I was so excited the day I boarded the plane to fly to the event. At last my prayers were answered, and life was good…at least until the next morning at 7:50 AM.

The Surprise

I was to be the opening 8:00 AM keynote speaker. The day's schedule was packed from early morning to evening with sessions running every hour to be presented by a host of different speakers. At 7:50 AM I began to get a little nervous as the crowd had not yet arrived. I busied myself at my book table—not that the table was busy, but shifting and straightening these books gave me someplace to release my nervous energy. I smiled at the other speakers doing the same thing. We all just shifted and straightened and smiled.

Then two people walked in, and suddenly a new step was added to our awkward dance. It became a four-step movement of shift, straighten, smile, and welcome. These two overly welcomed women were a bit shocked to have such ample choice of seating. They'd brought along Barbie umbrellas so they could signal their friends arriving a little later of their exact location in the large arena.

At 8 AM it was time to acknowledge the big elephant in the room. Two people were in the arena, and about 4998 people were missing!

The attendees tucked their umbrellas underneath their seats and busied themselves with a nervous dance of their own. Theirs was a two-step of sorts: chat and look. They'd chat a while and then look around the arena. I think we all kept thinking that these silly little nervous dances would somehow woo people to come and fill the place and we'd proceed on with the conference as planned. But it was not to be.

God Was Not Surprised

The time continued to pass with not much improvement. At 10:30 our crowd reached its peak of 12 ladies. Determined to make the best of an odd situation, one of the other speakers and I took charge. We asked the ladies to help us move folding chairs into the lobby, where they could sit in a circle while we delivered our messages. Soon it didn't matter how many people were there as we knew without a doubt that God was with us. We laughed, we cried, we ordered pizza, and we fulfilled God's purpose for that day. Our plans still didn't go perfectly as we were interrupted by the loud gospel band playing to an empty auditorium, so we decided to move our chairs out to the parking lot. Then came a sudden infestation of flies (I counted 17 on me at one time), a remote-controlled airplane flying over us that sounded like a dying cow, and of course rain. Hey, at least we made use of those Barbie umbrellas!

But God. I love this two-word phrase because life can literally be falling apart around us, *but God is good,* and no mess we find ourselves in can change that fact! Remember the little seed. Oh, how I wanted to resist God that day. I wanted to pack up my things and fly home. Many of the speakers did, but I knew God was telling me to stay in the hard place. Fulfill the mission in a God-honoring way. Love on these ladies who did come. Be okay with letting your dream die for today because life will eventually spring from it.

God is good. He is way more interested in developing our

characters to match our calling than in manipulating our circumstances to make us happy. God could have filled that arena that day. He could have changed all kinds of circumstances. But God's economy is different from our own. I told those 12 ladies that I believed that God had paused for us in this place to get all of our attention for different reasons, and He would use the circumstances of the day for great things.

Did I immediately see huge blessings from my cooperation with God? No. When the event coordinators came to pick my assistant and me up the next day to take us to the airport, conversation with them was awkward. I was still feeling a little shell-shocked by what had happened, and yet God was calling me to forgive their lack of planning, encourage them, and love them. So I did.

Did God immediately bless me for cooperating? Again, no. About an hour from the airport their car broke down, and my assistant and I wound up having to hitchhike to the airport! Once we were finally on the plane headed home, I didn't know whether to laugh or cry. To be honest I didn't know what to feel. The seed was cracking in the deep, dark place, and it hurt.

Being Broken Is Not Being Sidelined

Was this the death of my dream? Why would God plant a vision in my heart and then let it turn out like this? At times like this, I have to live my life based on the truth of who God says He is and not my feelings. My feelings were hurt, my heart was broken, and I couldn't process this event in a way that made me feel better. So I had to rely on the truth that God is good, He has every detail in His perfect control, and this will turn out okay; in the meantime, I can't rely on my emotional thinking. I must seek God's perspective. Even in my broken state, I had to press on seeking Him.

If you were to ask most people if they desired a life of extraordinary faith, they would probably say yes. So why aren't more people living out this desire? Because they confuse brokenness with being sidelined by God. Brokenness is what must happen before God can put the pieces back together in the way He can shine through the best.

The very first recorded sermon that Jesus gave to the crowds in the Bible is the Sermon on the Mount. We find it in Matthew 5, right after He tells His disciples in chapter 4 to "Come, follow me." So this was an important speech for Jesus. Though He'd been teaching and preaching throughout the land, this sermon must have held special importance and is the first time we get to hear Him word for word. Of all the topics He could have chosen to speak on, He spoke about brokenness.

Think about that. He had invited the disciples to leave everything and follow Him. He attracted quite a crowd. He was the talk of the town, the main attraction, the one everyone wanted to see. Can't you feel the excitement of the disciples? Can't you see their puffed-up chests and their confident stride? So Jesus pulls them close and rallies them with a real boost of self-confidence right?

No, He teaches them the importance of brokenness.

> Blessed are the poor in spirit…
>
> Blessed are those who mourn…
>
> Blessed are the meek…
>
> Blessed are those who hunger and thirst
> for righteousness…
>
> Blessed are the merciful…
>
> Blessed are the pure in heart…
>
> Blessed are the peacemakers…
>
> Blessed are those who are persecuted because of
> righteousness…(Matthew 5:3-10).

In all my years of reading these Scriptures, I read them as individual statements and missed an incredible insight. What if Jesus didn't mean for us to read them separately but rather as fluid stages of brokenness like this:

> Blessed are the poor in spirit...the broken people.
>
> Blessed are those who mourn...broken to the point of great weeping.
>
> Blessed are the meek...weeping to the point of being humbled past worldly things.
>
> Blessed are those who hunger and thirst for righteousness...humbled and desiring to be filled with God alone.
>
> Blessed are the merciful...filled with God and able to overflow mercy to others.
>
> Blessed are the pure in heart...freely extending mercy and living with a "yes" heart for God.
>
> Blessed are the peacemakers...saying yes to God and bringing His peace everywhere they go.
>
> Blessed are those who are persecuted because of righteousness...so certain in His peace that even when they face hardships, they trust and confidently walk with God no matter what.[6]

Beautiful, isn't it? Then Jesus goes on to say in verses 13-16, "You are the salt of the earth...the light of the world...let your light shine before men, that they may see your good deeds and praise your Father in heaven."

O Lord, thank You for shedding this new light on the beauty and value of brokenness. May I forever look at the broken places and experiences in my life in a new way. Thank You for loving me enough to save me from my ideas and desires. Only Your perfect way through brokenness can reveal the best road to travel. I know death doesn't surprise You, Lord, and brokenness doesn't mean an end. Praise You for new beginnings even when we can't see them yet. Thank You for the privilege of being broken enough to shine Your light through my life.

Personal Bible Study

1. Read Hosea 13:14; 1 Corinthians 15:55-57.

Jesus defeated death once and for all on the cross. God had a plan for our salvation so that none would perish (2 Peter 3:9). God, in His sovereignty, offered up His only Son so that we could be redeemed. Death did not surprise God then, and it does not now. Even when Jesus was on the cross, He was in control of death. In Luke 23:46, He says, "Father, into your hands I commit my spirit." John 19:30 says, "When He had received the drink, Jesus said, 'It is finished.' With that, He bowed His head and gave up His spirit." He chose the moment of His death. He was not really killed by those who crucified Him, nor was He surprised by His body's weakness. He chose to commit His spirit into God's hands. John 10:17-18 shows us that God is in control of all things—even death. Record your thoughts in your notebook.

2. Read 1 Thessalonians 5:1-11.

God is not surprised by death. In His mercy, He has provided us with a way not to be surprised by things of this world either. Verse 4 of this passage tells us, "But you, brothers, are not in darkness so that this day should surprise you like a thief." The passage goes on to tell us that we are "sons [and daughters] of the light" (verse 5). God has given us His light in our lives, and that light shines brightest when we are in His Word. He has given His Word to prepare us, to equip us, and to fit us for battle as described in verse 8. He loved us enough to reveal Himself to us so that we would not be surprised by the things of this world either. Commit in your heart to become better acquainted with the God of the universe through His Word. Look at Psalm 119 and list some of the things God's Word does for us.

3. Read Luke 19:10.

Jesus' mission was to build His kingdom by offering salvation to all who believe. The compelling truth about Jesus' dream was that He was willing to die for it. In fact, His death was the pivotal component of His dream. In order to achieve His desired outcome, He had to lay down His life. The Scriptures show us that He was human and felt the same emotions about dying that we would feel. Luke 22:42 tells us that Jesus decided to accept God's will—even to the point of death. Death was always part of God's plan to achieve His dream. Even though He may require death, you can trust His perfect plan for fulfilling His dream for you. God loves you and is always there. This truth is woven throughout Scripture. Take some time to reflect on these promises, and then go through the Bible and find promises that really speak to you. Write them down in your notebook and refer to these verses during this time. If you are doing this study with a group, share some of your verses as an encouragement to each other.

Sixteen

God's Portion,
Position, and Promise

I'VE HAD QUITE A WEEK WITH my sweet five-year-old, Brooke. Let me just give you a few of the highlights:

Miss Thing, as we affectionately call her, got in trouble at home for making a smart remark and had to be spanked. The next day, as I was getting ready in the bathroom, I spied her in the tub, giggling. When I asked her what was so funny, she replied, "Well, I promised myself I wouldn't tell you this, but I just can't help it. Before you spanked me yesterday, I put on five pair of underwear and the thickest pants I could find. I didn't even feel the spanking!" *What? My sweet Brooke...is she really that conniving?*

I had hardly recuperated from the spanking fiasco when my nine-year-old informed me that she caught Miss Thing shaving her legs with her daddy's razor. When I confronted Brooke about this, she smiled and said, "Mom, my legs are too hairy. I 'razored' them and didn't cut myself one time, so what's the big deal?" The big deal? "The big deal," I replied back, "is that you are five years old, and you will *not* be 'razoring' your legs. Not today, not tomorrow, not for years to come!" *My sweet Brooke...is she really that sneaky?*

Then came the real doozie! My babysitter had taken my girls to a jewelry store to pick up a charm bracelet we were giving as a gift. They weren't in the shop long before visions of her own charm bracelet started dancing through Miss Thing's mind. With her birthday just weeks away and Christmas only around the corner, it never occurred to her to simply ask for her own bracelet and wait for it to be given to her. She wanted a charm bracelet *now.* The sitter told her no, and we thought that was the end of that.

That is, until the next day, when her sister reached into the pocket of the pants Brooke had been wearing at the jewelry store and found eight silver charms inside! I marched her back up to the store, returned the charms, and made her apologize a most humble apology. With the store clerk's help, I also explained to Brooke that this incident could land her in jail and that the police would have to be called. After her brief conversation with a police officer, I felt sure this would be the end of her shoplifting days. *My sweet Brooke…is she really that apt to sin?*

The Cold Hard Fact

Where have I gone wrong as a mother? I mean, she's such a precious child—or at least she was a few days ago. But I had to face a cold hard fact. The easy answer would be to point the finger at myself and try a little harder to be a better parent. And I always have room for improvement, but that's not the whole answer. As much as I would like to think of Brooke as the sweet little angel she appears to be, I can't let her big blue eyes and wavy blond hair fool me. She is a sinner. She is infected with the same sin nature the rest of God's children are infected with—myself included. Without God, she would be left to her own bad decisions and faulty thinking. But with God, she has hope for a different kind of life.

When I study God's children, I feel much better about my own. Even He, the perfect Parent, had some pretty conniving, sneaky,

Sin - an immoral act

apt-to-sin kids! I must admit, in the past I have been quite harsh in my thinking about the children of Israel at times. I can't help but read their story and think, *You crazy fools! How could you see what you saw and experience what you experienced and still doubt and grumble against God!* The sad truth is that the same is true in my own life. I've had my own parting of the Red Sea, I've delighted in His provision time and again, and still I go my own way at times.

Just like the children of Israel and my sweet daughter Brooke, *I am a sinner.*

As long as we live on earth, we will sin. But sin doesn't have to rule us and ruin our lives. If we can remember a few lessons from the children of Israel, we'll be much better equipped to avoid the pitfalls of sin. Understanding God's portion, position, and promise will be key as we progress from the death phase to the sweet promised land of resurrection.

God's Portion

Not long after the children of Israel saw the parting of the Red Sea and witnessed the dead bodies of their enemies washing up on shore, they forgot God's amazing ability to provide. In Exodus 15:21 we find songs of praise to the Lord: "Sing to the LORD, for he is highly exalted. The horse and its rider he has hurled into the sea." But just three verses later, the praises have faded from their lips, and in their place we find a very different tune. "So, the people grumbled…" (Exodus 15:24). And they continued grumbling though God promised to take care of them and provide for them.

Psalm 78:22-25 says, "For they did not believe in God or trust in his deliverance. Yet he gave a command to the skies above and opened the doors of the heavens; he rained down manna for the people to eat, he gave them the grain of heaven. Men ate the bread of angels; he sent them all the food they could eat."

Though they didn't deserve His provision, God still had mercy on them and provided. The way He provided required them to pursue a relationship with Him on a daily basis, receiving their portion every day. God continued to reveal Himself to His people through the manner in which He provided. He still does this with us as well.

The Big Lie

I think one of the biggest tools Satan uses to keep people from growing in their faith and following after the dreams God has placed in their hearts is the lie that we have to do everything right before God will pay attention to us. We have to pray long and lofty prayers. We have to set aside chunks of time in the wee hours of dawn to do in-depth Bible study. We have to have a seminary-level knowledge of the Bible and be able to do expository preaching on any and every subject that might come up in our conversations with others. Once we reach this pinnacle in our faith, then God sits up, takes note of our devotion, and pays attention to us.

No! That's not the way it works!

Yes, God wants us to pray, read our Bible, and tell others about Him. But He wants us to do those things as a natural response of a heart that delights in our relationship with Him. God loves each of us and wants to spend time with us, not because it's on our to-do list but because we desire to stay in contact with Him throughout our day. He wants to be there for us. He wants to fill in the gaps where each of us falls short.

Our Weakness

When Paul pleaded with God to remove his "thorn," God refused and said, "My grace is sufficient for you, for my power is made perfect in your weakness." Paul goes on to say, "Therefore I will boast all the more gladly about my weaknesses, so that Christ's power may rest on me. That is why, for Christ's sake, I delight in weaknesses, in insults, in hardships, in persecutions, in difficulties. For when I am weak, then I am strong" (2 Corinthians 12:9-10).

Along the same line, God provided for the children of Israel in a way that made them admit their weakness and God's ability to provide. "Then the LORD said to Moses, 'I will rain down bread from heaven for you. The people are to go out each day and gather enough for that day. In this way I will test them and see whether they will follow my instructions. On the sixth day they are to prepare what they bring in, and that is to be twice as much as they gather on the other days'" (Exodus 16:4-5).

Every day the Israelites had to actively receive their portion. I have learned to do the same. Wherever I'm feeling weak, unable, or inadequate, I ask God to be my portion and fill in my gaps. Whether I run short on patience with my kids, love for my husband, forgiveness for someone who hurt me, or one of a myriad of other ways I sometimes miss the mark, I wake up in the morning and start my day by asking God for my portion of what I need.

We find these "portion" prayers throughout the Bible. Psalm 73:26: "My flesh and my heart may fail, but God is the strength of my heart and my portion forever." Lamentations 3:22-24: "Because of the LORD's great love we are not consumed, for his compassions never fail. They are new every morning; great is your faithfulness. I say to myself, 'The Lord is my portion; therefore I will wait for him.'" Even Jesus, when teaching us the Lord's prayer, prayed for His portion: "Give us today our daily bread" (Matthew 6:11). If He had to pray for His portion, why would we think that we wouldn't have to?

Wherever you are falling short, ask God to be your portion and fill in your gaps. Then watch for His hand at work and thank Him for the many ways He'll reveal Himself to you each day!

God's Position

God not only wants us to rely on Him for our daily portion but He also demands we keep first place in our lives reserved for Him.

It's easy to get so consumed with our promised land that we forget the promise Maker. We lose sight of the fact that God planted this dream in our heart and *He will surely carry it through to fruition.*

> You shall have no foreign god among you; you shall not bow down to an alien god. I am the LORD your God, who brought you up out of Egypt. Open wide your mouth and I will fill it. But my people would not listen to me; Israel would not submit to me. So I gave them over to their stubborn hearts to follow their own devices. If my people would but listen to me, if Israel would follow my ways, how quickly I would subdue their enemies and turn my hand against their foes! (Psalm 81:9-14).

> But their idols are silver and gold, made by the hands of men. They have mouths but cannot speak, eyes, but cannot see; they have ears but cannot hear; noses, but cannot smell; they have hands, but cannot feel; feet, but they cannot walk; nor can they utter a sound with their throats. Those who make them [idols] will be like them, and so will all who trust in them (Psalm 115:4-8).

Ask yourself this question: *What do I want more than anything else?* If your answer is anything other than *more of God in my life,* then you are worshiping an idol of some sort. Ask God to reveal to you the idols of your life, and turn back to Him.

> He feeds on ashes, a deluded heart misleads him; he cannot save himself, or say, "Is not this thing in my right hand a lie?" Remember these things, O Jacob, for you are my servant, O Israel. I have made you, you are my servant; O Israel, I will not forget you. I have swept away your offenses like a cloud, your sins like the morning mist. Return to me, for I have redeemed you (Isaiah 44:20-22).

God's Promise

Honestly, sometimes I get tired of the constant battles in my life. I hardly get one issue resolved when another seems to pop up. Not that I go looking for trouble, but somehow it always seems to find me. I've learned to view troubles in my life as "growth opportunities." They give me a chance to recognize God shaping and molding me to fit the calling He's given to me. God is interested in my character, not my comfort.

Last year, my girls and I went to a silversmith's workshop. When we walked into the shop, I was impressed by this man's artistic ability. His pieces were magnificently beautiful. They were so pure and smooth that I could see my reflection perfectly. Only when we went into the workroom did I understand what it took to get the silver to look as it had in the showroom. The pounding, turning, heating, and pounding some more gave me a new respect for all that silver must endure to be showroom quality. For that silversmith to put his name on a piece, it had to submit to treatment we might say is harsh and cruel. But I dare say the silver in the showroom would say it was worth it.

Max Lucado describes the process this way:

> Heating, pounding. Heating, pounding. Deadlines, traffic. Arguments, disrespect. Loud sirens, silent phones. Heating, pounding. Heating, pounding. Did you know that the *smith* in silversmith comes from the old English word *smite*? Silversmiths are professional smiters. So is God...God guards those who turn to him. The pounding you feel does not suggest his distance, but proves his nearness. Trust his sovereignty.[7]

God allows the heating and pounding, the abrasive rubs and polishing in my life for a reason. They are purifying and smoothing me so I will reflect Him. "The LORD will perfect that which concerns me" (Psalm 138:8 NKJV). "My Father is always at his work" (John 5:17). In the same way, God spent time molding and refining the children of Israel as well.

The Desert and the Promise

His promise was to deliver them to the promised land. God kept His promise as He keeps all His promises. But they didn't get there as quickly as they would have liked. Their disobedience and need to deepen their relationship with God kept them in the desert for 40 years. Maybe you feel like you're wandering in a desert of your own. Maybe you are wondering, while you're wandering, where God is and what He's up to. Maybe you feel frustrated with God and feel as though your desert experience is just a waste of time.

Rest assured, God is working in you just as the silversmith works with his silver. But He's also working around and about you. Just as an actor must spend time learning his lines and getting familiar with his part, you've got to learn your part as well. God is building the stage, perfecting the sets, and gathering the audience. Don't rush through what God intends for you to learn today. Stay close to Him, be open to His teachings, be faithful in the rehearsals—opening night is on its way.

God was around and about the children of Israel while they were wandering in the desert as well. But their frustration and grumbling prompted Moses' warning in Deuteronomy 6:10-12:

> When the LORD brings you into the land he swore to your fathers, to Abraham, Isaac, and Jacob, to give you—a land with large, flourishing cities you did not build, houses filled with all kinds of good things you did not provide, wells you did not dig, and vineyards and olive groves you did not plant—then when you eat and are satisfied, be careful you do not forget the LORD, who brought you up out of Egypt, out of the land of slavery.

What would be more important for the children of Israel to do, build cities or build a solid relationship with God? Fill houses or fill their hearts with more of God? Dig wells or dig into God's truths and let them change their attitudes? Plant vineyards and olive groves or let their own roots grow deep and steadfast as people of God?

Their death phase in the desert was actually a gift. It provided time to spend with God and to grow in their relationship with Him. In the meantime, God was setting the stage. He was preparing their promised land while teaching His children to learn to simply love and trust Him. "Trust in the LORD with all your heart and lean not on your own understanding; in all your ways acknowledge him, and he will make your paths straight" (Proverbs 3:5-6).

O child of God, let Him be your daily *portion*. Esteem only Him in your life and keep the Lord's *position* as number one in your life. And watch as He always has and always will keep His glorious *promises!* The death phase is coming to a close, and your resurrection is near...

Personal Bible Study

1. The portion: Read John 1:12-13; 1 John 5:4-5; Revelation 2:17.

When we read in the Old Testament about God sending manna from heaven for the Israelites, we might think that's just a nice old story that doesn't really apply to us today. These New Testament verses help us to see that God is still providing manna to His children. This manna doesn't visibly fall from the sky, but it's no less available to us as Christ's followers. As these verses tell us, we are overcomers when we become children of God.

The Israelites were God's chosen children, but we are also His children through Jesus' sacrifice and God's mercy. As part of God's family, He gives us hidden manna, which refers to the sufficiency of Christ for the believers' needs. May we all become more intentional about allowing Christ to be our portion of manna for each day. Write a prayer asking for God's provision in a particular area of your life.

2. The position: Read Habakkuk 2:18-20.

What exactly are idols? In Old Testament times they were graven images carved from wood or stone as described in these verses. But today idols can take many different forms. An idol is anything that becomes a barrier to your relationship with Christ. *Anything.* Even those precious children He has blessed you with. Even very worthwhile pursuits like volunteering or homeschooling can become idols if they take priority over God in your heart.

Now read Judges 6:25-32. This passage describes Gideon's first directive from God after he was called to deliver the people. Why did God require this of him?

I think God wanted an outward sign of Gideon's inner devotion to the Lord. This was accomplished by physically tearing down his father's altar and replacing it with an altar for God. God wants us to do the same. We may not need to smash the TV with a baseball bat, but we may need to drastically reduce the amount of time we spend in front of it. We may not need to give up our dreams, but we must *surrender* the dream. We should place the dream squarely *behind* God on our priority list.

In Matthew 6:33, Jesus reminds us to "seek first His kingdom and His righteousness, and all these things will be given to you as well." Spend some time in prayer, asking God to reveal the idols in your life to you. Record one of them in your notebook and write down how you can restore proper perspective in your life.

3. The promise: Read Exodus 15:13.

When we are in a desert time, we might think God is absent and begin to doubt His promise to us. We wonder, *Did He really call me to this?* and *Did I really hear that from Him?*

Losing our focus is easy when the desert seems so vast and endless. In this time we must focus on God's covenant of unfailing love. The Hebrew word for this love is *hesed,* which means loyal, steadfast, unfailing love. His love is there for us—working out His plans for us, protecting us, and guarding us as we make our way through the desert. Take a moment to thank God for His *hesed* for you today. Record your thanks in your notebook.

PHASE FIVE

Resurrection

Seventeen

God's Dream, God's Way

RESURRECTION—THE FINAL STAGE in our walk of faith—happens only after death has had her fleeting reign of victory. In other words, the only way to rejoice in the resurrection is to have sorrowed through death first.

Strange, isn't it? To the soul who has a lesser trust in God, the death phase could almost seem cruel and unnecessary. But the closer we walk with the Lord, the more we start rejoicing in it. For we've come to recognize this as the sign that the new life we desperately desire and can't get any other way is just around the corner.

And the death makes us people who can accept the accolades of resurrection without pride. Remembering the death phase keeps us humble and keenly aware that the resurrection has nothing to do with us. Our talents, our creativity, our manipulating, our arranging, our being in the right place at the right time—*none of it brought about the good that is dawning.*

God's dream planted in us is brought about by *His* hand alone. Only now can we let credit go to where credit is due. Not by our own efforts but by God's grace did this happen, and that we now know full well.

God's dream for us must come to life God's way.

A Resurrection Story

My dream of writing a book had to die before it could finally come to life. My efforts to solve the problem with my neighbor had to fail for me to see God's hand providing His beautiful provision. My thoughts of what my family would look like had to die so that a dream I didn't even know I had could bring the joy of my adopted sons. My suggestion to God for an arena event had to flop miserably before God's plan could be revealed. Yes, even that escapade has a resurrection story.

After I returned home from that most humbling of experiences, I have to admit, I felt weary, insecure, and vulnerable. And that was a good thing, for that very week I went to the concert where I first met my Liberian boys. God humbled me and taught me a lot through the failed conference, but He also helped me to be especially sensitive. He could easily speak to me the night of that concert because I had just been broken.

I was broken and humbled enough to no longer desire worldly things. I wanted to be filled with God alone, living with a "yes" heart for Him, bringing mercy and peace to others in a way I could not have otherwise. But there was even more to the end of this story than that.

My assistant, who had been with me at the arena event, was burdened for the couple who had arranged the conference. They were now in debt in a big way. They owed thousands of dollars to the arena, the musicians, the speakers, and other businesses involved with the conference. Repaying the debt would take a miracle. I figured I would never see the balance of my speaker fee or a reimbursement of my plane fare, and I made peace with that fact and moved on.

Not Fair!

But my assistant couldn't let it go. She prayed for this couple. She tried to figure out a way to help them. She sought out a donor to help dig them out of their financial hole. Finally, she prevailed and was reeling with joy as she told me how she was going to be able to help. There was only one catch. I had to forgive the part of the debt owed to me, and then the rest would be paid. She looked at me with a questioned expression and said, "That will be all right with you, won't it?"

I considered this. Every other speaker was going to get paid, but not me. No one else, not even the irresponsible planners of this event, would suffer financially from this event, but I would. I suddenly felt as if I were eight years old and being punished for something my sister did. I put on the biggest pout I could and looked right up in the direction I assumed God's face might be and said...nothing.

Though my flesh wanted to scream, "Not fair! Not fair! Not fair!" God's Spirit inside me made me pause for just a minute. Remembering God's faithfulness time and time again, I silently prayed. *God, this isn't fair, but I don't need to tell You that. So I'm choosing to honor You here for no other reason than that I love You.*

"Yes," I replied. "Of course I will forgive my part of their debt." I willed my mouth to say it. I wanted to honor God even when my flesh screamed for me to do otherwise. And trust me, my feelings took a while to catch up, but eventually they did.

Though I'd made a different choice many times before, this time I chose wisely. It felt good. It felt freeing. It felt enabling. Somehow, this time, I'd battled the evil desires within me and won. Romans 12:1 says, "Therefore, I urge you, brothers, in view of God's mercy, to offer your bodies as living sacrifices, holy and pleasing to God—this is your spiritual act of worship."

Your Promised Land Is Close

In other words, in light of all the mercy God had extended to me, which is quite considerable, this sacrifice was small. This was an opportunity to offer my desires as a sacrifice. One that was holy, or "set apart." This was a sacrifice that couldn't be understood by worldly wisdom but that truly pleased God. In doing this, I worshiped God, and in that He would delight.

Psalm 37:4 says, "Delight yourself in the LORD and he will give you the desires of your heart." The very day I released the debt, a most amazing thing happened. I received an invitation to speak at a real arena event. And not just one. I am now under contract to do five events for these new sponsors.

The resurrection may seem to have happened immediately, but it did not. God had other things that needed to happen first. Opportunities for me to be obedient before I even hoped for a resurrection of the very thing my heart desired. Worth noting here is the fact that the resurrection didn't happen until the debt was released.

Are you in a waiting period right now? Though your resurrection may not happen as quickly as you would like, it is coming. Your promised land is close. In the meantime, look for opportunities to honor the Lord today. Look for an opportunity to release a debt, forgive someone who has hurt you, or choose to bless the one cursing you. Resist the urge to feel angry, disillusioned, or jealous of those who seem to have the very thing you keep waiting on. Determine to bless the one you are angry with, encourage the one who discourages you, and cheer for someone you are feeling jealous toward. Doing these things will break the downward spiral you will otherwise be pulled into.

Strength in God's Promises

Doing these things would be impossible on your own, but God's promises will give you the strength. Romans 12:14,21 says, "Bless those who persecute you; bless and do not curse...Do not be overcome with evil but overcome evil with good." Your good choices will cause Satan to flee...flee from you and flee from your situation. Isn't that what you desire?

Second Peter 3:9 says, "The Lord is not slow in keeping his promise, as some understand slowness. He is patient with you, not wanting anyone to perish, but everyone to come to repentance." This verse is actually referring to Jesus' return, but look at the reason for the delay: His patience. He is waiting for His people to get ready. In the same way, He is being patient with you in this waiting period as well. Like any good parent, God is desiring to make good things happen for you, but He won't do it until you are ready to receive them.

Thank God for Saying No

As I write this, I'm sitting in a Barnes and Noble bookstore. A child is screaming from the back of the store, "I want it! I want it now! I want it, want it, want it!" My friend with me just looked up and smiled as we were having the exact same thoughts. If that mom gives in and lets the child have whatever he wants right now, he'll stop screaming, but he'll never appreciate what he's been given. If, however, this mom perseveres, the child stands to learn some very valuable lessons:

- "No" doesn't mean the world comes to an end. It simply means not now, not yet, not necessary, or not in your best interest.

- If you wait for what your heart desires, you treasure it more when you finally do get it.

- Kicking and screaming and having a bad attitude while you wait is no fun for you or for those around you.

- Getting the thing you want might be the worst thing for you.

Sometimes I think we are very much like that screaming child. I thank God for the nos and the not yets in my life. Though they may not be what I want, they are exactly what I need. God is getting me ready to receive the promised land.

I must learn to be content in His provision today. Think back to the story of the manna in our last section. God was faithful to provide the children of Israel just enough of His portion for each day. But like that screaming child, one day they demanded more. Dissatisfaction came as they focused on what they didn't have instead of what they did have:

> The rabble with them began to crave other food, and again the Israelites started wailing and said, "If only we had meat to eat! We remember the fish we ate in Egypt at no cost—also the cucumbers, melons, leeks, onions and garlic. But now we have lost our appetite; we never see anything but this manna!" (Numbers 11:4-6).

Does that sound like a child in need of some serious discipline or what?

Notice the word "rabble." These were the mixed crowd of Egyptians and others who followed along with Israel out of Egypt. God could take the people out of Egypt, but He had to discipline the Egypt out of them. And discipline them, He did. "Now the LORD will give you meat, and you will eat it. You will not eat it for just one day, or two days, or five, ten or twenty days, but for a whole month—until it comes out of your nostrils and you loathe it—because you have rejected the LORD, who is among you, and have wailed before him" (Numbers 11:18-20).

The people didn't ask God to fill their real need—their ache within. They came up with their own solution and demanded it now. They got what they asked for, and as we later learn in Numbers 11:33-34, it became the death of them. So close to the resurrection, they let evil consume their hearts in their waiting time and missed the promised land entirely.

God's dream must be experienced God's way. If you settle for anything else, you'll never be satisfied. "Yet the LORD longs to be gracious to you; he rises to show you compassion. For the LORD is a God of justice. Blessed are all who wait for him!" (Isaiah 30:18).

Personal Bible Study

1. Read Psalm 27:13-14; 33:20; 40:1; 130:5-8.

As we read these verses, we see that David struggled with waiting as much as we all do. It's not easy to wait on God when we want to move forward. We think we know how things should turn out, and we want to see resolution. These verses show us ten things we can do while we are waiting. A friend of mine calls this "actively waiting."

1. Do not lose confidence in God's goodness.
2. Be strong.
3. Do not lose hope.
4. Let God be your shield and your help.
5. Be patient.
6. Continue to cry out to God.
7. Cling to His Word.
8. Watch for His answers.
9. Trust in His unfailing love.
10. Rejoice in His redemption.

Continue to practice these ten things as you wait for the resurrection that will surely follow death.

What are you waiting for? How will this help you?

2. Read Matthew 6:9-13.

Most of us are familiar with this passage, having recited it or sung it countless times. But have we read it from the Bible and really applied it to our own prayer life recently? When we are in a time of waiting, we can communicate with the Lord and cry out to Him as the psalmist said. Jesus taught us how to pray in this passage. Verse 12 stood out to me: "Forgive us our debts as we also have forgiven our debtors." I thought of my assistant asking me to cancel my debt, and I remembered Christ went to the cross to cancel mine.

Write out a personal prayer using the Lord's Prayer as a guide. Using the key points from the verses you have read, begin with these phrases:

> Lord, I praise You for…
>
> Help me to do Your will by…
>
> Lord, I need…
>
> Please forgive me for…
>
> And help me to forgive…
>
> I am struggling with…
>   please help me to stand firm.
>
> For You alone are Lord, and I give You all the glory.
> Amen.

3. Read Psalm 16:2; 73:25; Philippians 3:8.

Though we will never arrive at a point of spiritual perfection, we must remember that these three verses are our goal. As we journey with God, we should desire nothing more than to fellowship with Him. Anything that you desire more than that is an idol. Knock it down just as Gideon tore down the altar. Is there still something in your life that is more desirable than God? If you can, write about it in your notebook and then ask God to help you tear down that barrier to Him in your life.

Eighteen

A Promise Made
Is a Promise Kept

ABOUT SIX MONTHS BEFORE I MET my two sons from Africa, I wrote this in my journal:

> Sometimes I get overwhelmed with all the ministry opportunities that surround me every day. Children are starving in distant lands, a single mom is struggling financially down the street, a crisis pregnancy center in town needs volunteers, and friends from church could use a home-cooked meal brought to their home. I see homeless shelters and battered women's homes and people in dire situations who walk the streets of my city every day.
>
> We live in a fallen world, where people's circumstances belie what God meant for His people to be and become. Yet here I sit in a warm home with a pantry stocked full of food and three little people who are looking at the way I live and patterning their lives after mine. This thought pounds in my head: *I am only one person, I have three small children, limited resources, and an already full schedule. What can I do? I can't right all the wrongs of this world.*

I can't possibly help all the helpless. So I turn my head and do nothing.

Oh sure, I serve through Proverbs 31 Ministries and in my local church body, but what about the helpless? What about those who truly have nothing and nobody to turn to? Who will be Jesus to them today? Who will live out the biblical response to those in need?

James 2:14-17 says, "What good is it, my brothers, if a man claims to have faith but has no deeds? Can such faith save him? Suppose a brother or sister is without clothes and daily food. If one of you says to him, 'Go, I wish you well; keep warm and well fed,' but does nothing about his physical needs, what good is it? In the same way, faith by itself, if it is not accompanied by action, is dead."

I am determined to stop turning my head. I vow that even though I cannot reach them all, I can reach one. God, show me which one.

A Daily Assignment

Not long after writing this, I heard of a little boy named Sergei living in an orphanage in Belarus (right below Russia). Through another family who adopted a son from this same orphanage, I was able to obtain photographs of the living conditions these boys face every day.

My heart broke. I wanted to do whatever I could do to help him, and I started praying for God's direction. Each day I asked God for an assignment to help Sergei. Some days I was to pray for him. Other days I would call and send e-mails, inquiring of the possibilities to let him travel to spend time in our home. Though I had limitations, God blessed my obedience and gave me assignments I could do.

I received one of my most precious assignments in the middle of the night. I woke up with tears streaming down my face. At first, I was confused and asked the Lord why I was crying. God gently touched my heart by answering, *You are taking Sergei's tears today. That is what you are doing in My Name to change the world today. One orphan will go to bed tonight without one single tear.*

God was certainly stirring something in my heart. These were more than just prayers for an orphan child; they were the beginning of new adventures with God. Something was awakening in my spirit. My heart was becoming more aware of how to beat in tandem with the Lord's heart. A resurrection of meaning and purpose and desire was dawning on my horizon.

Secret Service

All along this ministry journey, I kept thinking God was looking for me to do great things *for* Him. But now I am convinced the Lord isn't looking for a bestselling author or an arena speaker. He isn't looking for people to dance in the limelight. He is looking for those souls who are willing to press close to His heart and hear the cries of the forgotten. He wants us to do great things *with* Him to reach "the least of these." Ministry that makes the biggest impact is that which is done in the secret places, the hard stuff that is void of glory but full of guts. Theodore Roosevelt spoke of this kind of service:

> It is not the critic who counts: not the man who points out how the strong man stumbles or where the doer of deeds could have done better. The credit belongs to the man who is actually in the arena, whose face is marred by dust and sweat and blood, who strives valiantly...who knows the great enthusiasms, the great devotions, who spends himself for a worthy cause; who, at the best, knows, in the end, the triumph of high achievement, and who, at the worst, if he fails, at least fails while daring

greatly, so that his place shall never be with those cold and timid souls who knew neither victory nor defeat.[8]

A Promise Made...

I knew in my heart that to try adopting Sergei would be costly, extremely time-consuming, and risky. By this time, we'd already started adoption proceedings for our two sons from Africa. My face was already "marred by dust and sweat and blood," so to speak. Were we to take on this too?

As crazy as most of our family and friends thought we were, we decided to march on with all three adoptions—our two boys from Libera and now Sergei. Sergei's would be much more complicated than the other two, but God kept opening the doors, so we kept walking through them. The same weekend our boys from Africa came to live in our home permanently, Sergei arrived for his five-week Christmas visit. Life was loud and crazy and messy and more wonderful than ever before. As a matter of fact, Art and I never opened our presents. They seemed a little insignificant when we had more joy than we could contain just watching kids who'd never had anything experience the love of a family at Christmas.

Sergei's visit flew by, and before we knew it, the time had come for him to return to his orphanage halfway across the world. The day before he left, we asked an interpreter to help us discuss with Sergei the possibility of adopting him. He said he loved our family and wanted to be a part of it. We promised him we'd do everything in our power to complete the necessary paperwork to bring him home quickly, never dreaming it could take years.

"He Will Understand"

At the writing of this book, the process has already taken more than a year, and we still don't have him home. It has been a hard year of wanting and waiting, feeling hopeful and at the same time quite helpless. We've only been able to get a couple of packages to him, a few e-mails, and one phone call.

When we were working on arranging the phone call with Sergei, I asked some of the officials to please provide an interpreter to help facilitate our discussion. I wanted Sergei to know the adoption was being delayed not by us but rather by the red tape of two very different governments. When no interpreter was available, my heart sank. So much time had passed since Sergei had communicated in English with us, I doubted he would remember enough to make the conversation meaningful.

The lady helping to arrange the call, one of the few Christians involved on their end, knew I was disappointed with the news. So the day before the call was to take place, she sent me an e-mail to encourage me: "There will be no intrepreter as nobody knows English at Ryasno. But you will tell him that you love him, and that he will understand."

What a beautiful truth. Yes, I believe Sergei did remember my voice and understand that his mommy loves him. One of the first sentences Sergei spoke to me in English was "I love you, Mommy." The conversation was shorter than I would have liked and void of all the explanations I wanted to give him, but it was good. It was just the way God planned and probably all Sergei needed.

The Belarussian lady's comment reminds me so much of what God continues to teach me about trusting Him. When I grieve over the bummer things in life and cry out to God, I can imagine God instructing the Holy Spirit to say something similar to me. *There is no way to interpret this event in a way she can comprehend, but tell her that I love her, and that she will understand.*

Isn't God amazing? Yes indeed, God is good. Even when I can't understand His timing and His ways, I do fully understand His love, and that *is* enough.

A Promise Kept

No, God has not yet resurrected this situation the way I hope He will. But He has resurrected the way I now look at it. We may have to pass through the stages of faith many times before our sweet Sergei comes home, but the dream is worth the price. And what if God's final answer is no? With tears in my eyes I will say, like the hymn so beautifully states, it is still well with my soul. I will not see this as a waste of time and money. I will refuse to get bogged down in bitterness. I will feel privileged that I can know and love and pray for this boy. This boy, with whom I share no biological connection but who has captured my heart and tapped into my maternal instincts. This boy, whom I will forever love as I treasure our five short weeks together.

My favorite time with Sergei was at night after his bath, when I would come into his room and put him to bed. I would say prayers and tuck the blankets the way he liked, tight all around his small body with only the top of his head and eyes peeking out. Then I would sing him into dreamland and watch peace envelop this little life.

This is a picture I treasure. I feel certain that Sergei's soul was forever impacted by his time with us, and Jesus will someday come to be Lord of his life. Though he may not have the home here on earth I want him to, I'm convinced he'll have something far better: an eternal home with no more tears, no more hunger, no more lonely nights, no more uncertain days, no more dashed hopes, and no more unanswered questions.

Regardless of what happens, I've found peace in knowing that God has promised in Psalm 68:5 to be "a father to the fatherless." Even though the best answer seems to me to be having Sergei with us, truly the best place for him is where he can come to know God. Though a forgotten orphanage seems like an unlikely place, God is there. I can picture choirs of angels singing him to sleep and his heavenly Father tucking him into bed. As his eyes peek over the tightly wound covers, the last sight he'll see each night is his heavenly Daddy's smiling face.

And what about my promise to Sergei? My promise to come and get him will not be broken even if I never physically get to bring him home. For I taught Sergei about Jesus, the one his soul really longs for even more than a mommy and daddy. The most glorious part of the resurrection is the promise Jesus gave us that He will return. "Behold, I am coming soon!…Behold, I am coming soon! My reward is with me, and I will give to everyone according to what he has done. I am the Alpha and Omega, the First and the Last, the Beginning and the End…Yes, I am coming soon!" (Revelation 22:7,12,20).

I would be remiss if I led you to believe that on this faith journey, the resurrection phase always ends with "happily ever after." We live in a fallen world with gaps and gut-wrenching injustices. But our souls can rise above the dusty roads of this earth into the victorious heavenly realm that is our real home. We must always remember this place is but a stop along the way, not our real destination.

A Bible teacher once shared that FAITH stands for Forsaking All, I Trust Him. Numbers 23:19-20 says, "God is not a man, that he should lie, nor a son of man, that he should change his mind. Does he speak and then not act? Does he promise and not fulfill? I have received a command to bless; he has blessed, and I cannot change it."

He may not resurrect all of the circumstances in your life, but He will resurrect a deeper and more secure trust of Him if you will let Him.

Personal Bible Study

1. Read Luke 1:5-25; 18:1-8.

Zechariah was a very old man when an angel told him, "Do not be afraid...your prayer has been heard." By the time the angel appeared, Zechariah had probably given up on ever having his prayer for a child answered by God. He had gone on with his life, accepting God's silence as a no and continuing to serve the Lord. Luke 1:6 tells us both Zechariah and his wife, Elizabeth, were "upright in the sight of God, observing all the Lord's commandments and regulations blamelessly." They chose to continue to honor God and placed their relationship with Him above their need to have children. They chose not to become bitter and did not turn away from the Lord. Yet God, in His timing, chose to answer their prayers long after they expected Him to. Sometimes we stop praying, throw our hands up, and assume that our prayers will be forgotten just because we've stopped asking. This story shows us that God answers prayers according to His timing, not ours. May we not forget that essential element in our prayer life.

Jesus uses the parable of the widow and the judge to show us that we should always pray and not give up. Just as the widow eventually "wore out" the judge, so we can prevail upon God by persevering in our prayer life. Luke 18:7 says, "And will not God bring about justice for His chosen ones, who cry out to Him day and night? Will He keep putting them off?" Don't let worldly wisdom keep you from going before God continually with your needs. I have learned this as I have felt that I must be wearing God out with my continued prayers for Sergei. I will continue to pray expectantly and will only stop when I feel God answer. Galatians 4:18 says, "It is fine to be zealous, provided the purpose is good." May we all be zealous in our prayer life! Write down an area you may have given up on that you need to recommit to pray for.

2. Read Psalm 56:8; Isaiah 25:8; Revelation 7:17.

The night I woke up crying for Sergei, God brought these verses to mind. Though I took Sergei's tears on that one amazing night, God shows us in His Word that He takes our tears every day. How amazing to me that the God of the universe pauses in the midst of all His creation to wipe away our tears and save them in a bottle. The next time I cry, I plan to thank God through my tears that He cares about me that way—and He cares about you that way too! Record what these verses mean to you personally.

3. Read Romans 8:23-25.

As I've experienced the miracle of adoption firsthand, I've learned what a gift from God it is to be grafted into His family. Every soul longs to feel at home, and we are all groaning inwardly for our real home, heaven. There we will experience resurrection unlike any form of resurrection we have experienced on earth. We will take part in God's family in God's house. As the song goes, "What a day of rejoicing that will be." Thank God that He has adopted you into His family today.

Jeremiah 29:11
Phillipans 4:6-7

anxiety- aggitated ; high anxiety
tense, discouraged, confuse
doubtful, get ahead of
yourself

Keep saying it until it learns on
fertile ground - I trust you god

god will come into my spirit if I
invite Him

Nineteen

God Brings Dreams to Life

As the lady made her way toward me, I knew exactly what she was thinking and feeling. She felt so insignificant. So small. She made her way to me in the front of the room. I was surrounded by women of all ages. Some just wanted to give me a tearful hug. Others held my book in their hands, looking for a note of encouragement and an autograph. She just wanted to ask me *how?* How could she take a broken life and allow God to use it for His glory? Is it possible that a girl rejected by her earthly father could actually be chosen and set apart for a divine calling? How could she get past the place of not being able to make it through the day to proclaiming God's love from the podium?

She waited in line for her turn. Then, as she opened her mouth to speak, her throat tightened, her eyes filled with tears, and all she could squeak out was an emotional "how?" She wanted me to take her home with me and teach her. She wanted me to pack her in my suitcase and whisk her away from her life and into the life of one making a difference. She wanted me to share some quick and easy answer, three easy steps to the life you dream of, all for the low price of attending the seminar. But I wasn't a magician, a slick salesman, or a woman looking for a new houseguest. I was a woman who had experienced deep hurts and bitter disappointments, and who had chosen to surrender her life to God and was now being used by Him.

I did not give her the quick and easy answer she was looking for. I didn't give her any profound wisdom or direction. We only had time for me to simply tell her how I got started, and then she found herself making her way back to her seat. But she wasn't heading back empty and without hope.

I pray what I lacked in words, I made up for in example. I pray she had seen Jesus in me. I pray she had seen living proof of God's redemption. I pray she thought to herself, *If God could do that with her, I think there's hope for me after all.* And I pray something new and big and God-directed was born in her and confirmed in her heart in an undeniable way that day.

Though she still didn't know *how,* I pray she knew God could find a way. Though she didn't know *when,* I pray she now knew the timing was in His hands. Though she didn't even think she had much to offer, I knew God would fill in her gaps. I pray she simply knew God was calling her, inviting her, wooing her to something with His fingerprints all over it, and that would be enough.

Experiencing God

Remember the first chapter of the book? The same scene had happened many years before, only now I was the speaker. I could hardly believe it. God does bring dreams to life! I had just spoken to an auditorium filled with women and to more than 100,000 via simulcast. My book table was stacked high with my books, and now women were lining up to meet me. That's when it hit me.

This is not what fills my heart with joy. I was humbled to be a vessel through which other women could be touched. I was thankful to be able to experience all this. But it simply was not the pinnacle experience I always thought it would be. It didn't make me feel more significant or less insecure. It was fleeting, and the glimmer of limelight was quite empty. The realization hit me hard: The joy of the journey is not simply reaching the promised land. The real joy was experiencing God throughout all the phases of faith. I closed my eyes and drank in this moment of truth.

We are amazingly similar to the children of Israel. We spend half our lives looking back at our own Egypt with selective memories, longing to have our comfort zone back. Then we spend the other half wishing our days away for a dreamy future in our own promised land. The short time we actually focus on today's journey is often wasted on complaining, grumbling, wishing to be in a different place, or simply and mindlessly going through the motions of life. Why do we struggle with embracing the moment we've been given and experiencing God in the here and now?

Regardless of where you are today, God is with you. God is wooing you. God wants you to experience Him. Whatever you are going through today, you can find His joy and peace. However distant your dreams may seem, God is working things out, and today is an important part of that process. Remember your experiences with God. Write them down. Ponder them often. Treasure them in your heart. And vow to make experiencing God the highest goal of your faith journey. ✳

Shortcuts

Neither the journey nor the promised land will give my heart what it truly desires. I have to walk with God daily and let Him have His way in my heart. I have to embrace the struggles as well as the triumphs, the joys and the sorrows, the deaths and the resurrections. No shortcut or quick fix will help me become the woman God wants me to become.

Some time ago, Art thought he would take a shortcut of sorts. Through the wonders of modern technology, the wonderful LASIK eye surgery held great promise to rid Art of his dreaded contacts and glasses. But he wanted to get it done cheaper and faster than most of the doctors in our area could promise, so he put the surgery off. Then one day, he spotted a coupon in our paper for a superfast, supercheap LASIK surgery, and he jumped at the opportunity.

I was a bit concerned the day of the surgery when I arrived at the medical facility. Whoever heard of having surgery on your eyes done in the back of a truck parked on the side of a shopping center near the dumpster! But the lure of saving a few bucks and getting a quick fix negated the doubts Art might have been having, and he walked up the wobbly stairs and disappeared into the truck.

At first, the surgery seemed to have worked. But as the months wore on, Art's eyesight went right back to being as bad as before, if not a little worse. He eventually had to drive out of town to a specialist to get his eyes worked on again, which wound up costing him more time and money than if he'd just had it done right in the first place.

But I can't fault Art for his medical escapade because I've made the same mistake in my spiritual walk so many times. You know about many of my experiences because you've read about them in this book. My times of running ahead of God, making suggestions to Him, manipulating circumstances, and feeling frustrated when my shortcuts…well, fell short! I get a vision for something, make a beeline toward making it happen, and request that God would bless my plans. How that must break His heart.

Our Driving Force

There is an eternal purpose to all of this that cannot be left out.

> There dwells inside you, deep within, a tiny whippoorwill. Listen. You will hear him sing…We forget he is there, so easy he is to ignore. Other animals of the heart are larger, noisier, more demanding, more imposing. But none is so constant. Other creatures are more quickly

fed. More simply satisfied. We feed the lion who growls for power. We stroke the tiger who demands affection. We bridle the stallion who bucks control. But what do we do with the whippoorwill that yearns for eternity?[9]

Have you heard this constant chirping in your soul? Little reminders that this place is not all there is? I'm so thankful the earth will always produce discontentments and shortcomings. I'm so grateful that speaking before crowds of people isn't all that it's cracked up to be. I'm thrilled to get to know other speakers I've long admired and realize they don't really have it any more together than I do. Because all this keeps my heart centered and grounded on God alone. We must learn to long for the one who holds our eternity and let His song be the driving force in our heart.

Hall of Fame

Pursuing a deeper faith isn't about playing the spiritual game of keeping up with the Joneses, being admired and commended for our great spiritual acquisitions. No, quite the opposite. Walking closely with God gives us a more keen insight of our desperate need for Him.

Think for just a minute about the person who has been the greatest spiritual influence on your life. She could be a well-known Bible teacher or a lady in your church. Whoever it is, let me let you in on a little secret. She still struggles with insecurity every now and then. There are things about her life she has tried for years to change and still can't. She has people in her life who bug her and rub her the wrong way. God has even hurt her feelings a time or two. Oh, gasp! She is so human.

Hebrews 11, faith's hall of fame, commends many people for the way they walked with God. But as I scan these verses, I can't help but be struck by the reality that each and every person listed had some faults. None of them lived perfect lives, but they did live lives worthy of being mentioned in God's Word. Why? Well, it had very little to do with them at all. They were listed simply because they believed God is who He said He is, and they trusted He would do what He said He would do. "Faith is being sure of what we hope for and certain of what we do not see. This is what the ancients were commended for" (Hebrews 11:1-2).

As I've said over and over, the important thing is not what you do for God but rather that you come to know and believe Him along the way.

Personal Bible Study

1. Read Acts 7:44-50.

As we've gone through this story of God's people from Abraham to Joshua, we have continually seen God in the midst of His people. Does He *need* a tabernacle or sanctuary on earth? No. As these verses tell us, He has all of heaven as His throne, and the earth is merely His footstool. He does not need us to build Him a place to rest. But He knew that we would need a place to meet with Him—a visual reminder that He is in our midst.

Our creator knows what we need. In His mercy, He gave the Israelites that visual reminder by instructing them to build the tabernacle. Today, the church, the Bible, and even our own homes can serve as visual reminders of God's presence. Jesus is accessible to us at all times. He came as Emmanuel, God *with* us. He tore the veil that separates us from God. Through His death, He is always in our midst, and we are never alone. Praise the Lord today for being Emmanuel in your life—and don't forget that He is there for you always. Write down ways that you can make your home a sanctuary.

One suggestion: go back through this book and pick out Scriptures that have impacted you. Write them on index cards and place them around your home. Deuteronomy 6:9 says, "Write them on the doorframes of your houses and on your gates."

2. Read Psalm 78:4-7; 79:13.

This chapter is called "God Brings Dreams to Life." As you have taken the journey through this book and the Bible study, you have undoubtedly had some amazing encounters with the Lord. You have seen God bring dreams to life regardless of what point of the journey you are in. Be careful to remember your experiences with God and pass them along to the next generation as these verses describe.

In the days and weeks to come, make an effort to share some part of your story with someone. If you have children, share with them, in a way that they can understand, what you have been learning about God. Tell them about the dreams that God has planted in your heart and how God is working them out in your life. Reassure them that *they* are part of your dreams. By doing this, you make God real to them. They learn by example that they too can have a relationship with God. When Moses handed down the Ten Commandments to the Israelites, he told the people, "These commands that I give to you today are to be upon your hearts. Impress them on your children. Talk about them when you sit at home and when you walk along the road, when you lie down and when you get up" (Deuteronomy 6:6-7). Talk to your kids and to your loved ones about God. Make His name famous in your home. Write down some ideas of specific stories you can share with others about God's work in your life. Ask God to bring some to mind if you are struggling with this.

3. Read Exodus 17:14-15; Joshua 4:1-9.

Both of these passages talk about setting up some sort of memorial to what God has done in our lives. Whether we write it down as a remembrance, make a banner, or build an altar, we are memorializing God's work in our lives for all to see. God obviously feels that this is important for us to do because He included these and other examples in the Bible. How can you create a remembrance of what God has done in your life? Ask Him to reveal a way that perfectly suits your unique personality and giftedness. Write down some ideas in your notebook.

Twenty

Every Promise Fulfilled

Wow, what an adventure we have been on! And what unlikely people we've seen rise to be the starring members of the cast for this show. God first planted the dream of a chosen nation of people coming from a childless man named Abraham. Then on to Joseph, who spent a good bit of his life being betrayed and living in prison but then rose to be the second most powerful man in the world. And we must not forget Moses, who not only saw some of the most amazing miracles ever performed by the hand of God but also saw God Himself! Then it was on to the children of Israel, whose cycles of disobedience proved to be rich training ground for us. Now, finally, the moment we've all been waiting for—Joshua and the promised land!

Joshua inspires me like no other character in the Bible because of his determination to be absolutely obedient to God. He threw aside all his human reservations and followed hard after God. He was with Moses in Egypt through all the ups and downs of wandering in the desert, and saw his beloved leader die before reaching the promised land. He observed and learned well. Now his time to lead had come. But he did not hesitate like Moses. He did not question God as Moses did. God said it, Joshua believed it, and the promised land was conquered.

Look at the profoundly different ways Moses and Joshua approached the tasks set before them.

Their Confidence

When God told Moses he'd be the leader, Moses looked at all the reasons he couldn't do it. We see no similar record of Joshua hesitating. Joshua must have known his calling had very little to do with his qualifications. God would be the deliverer. Joshua understood and walked confidently in that knowledge.

God had said, "No one will be able to stand up against you all the days of your life. As I was with Moses, so I will be with you; I will never leave you nor forsake you. Be strong and courageous, because you will lead these people to inherit the land I swore to their forefathers to give them" (Joshua 1:5-6). What a confidence-building statement from God!

God went on to tell him to be "strong and courageous" two more times in this chapter. God even had the Israelites reassure him the same way, "Whatever you have commanded us we will do, and wherever you send us we will go. Just as we fully obeyed Moses, so we will obey you. Only may the LORD your God be with us as he was with Moses. Whoever rebels against your word and does not obey your words, whatever you command them, will be put to death. Only be strong and courageous!" (Joshua 1:16-18).

Did Joshua's confidence come as a natural by-product of his personality? I don't think so. If confidence came naturally to Joshua, I don't think God would have had to tell him to be strong and courageous over and over again. No, Joshua's confidence was steadfast because he was confident in God's promises.

Their Boldness

Israel fled from Egypt under Moses' lead, but they panicked

when they reached the Red Sea. They were trapped between a deadly army and a dangerous sea. Moses cried out to the Lord on their behalf and told the people to just stand still. God seemed frustrated when He replied, "Why are you crying out to me? Tell the Israelites to move on. Raise your staff and stretch out your hand over the sea to divide the water so that the Israelites can go through the sea on dry ground." Perhaps God had already said to move on and no one moved. Not even a toe was put into the water until the waters parted first and the ground was dry.

In contrast, when God instructed Joshua to tell the priests to go into the Jordan River, they did so without hesitation. Under Joshua's leadership they were willing to get wet and trust God to part the water before they saw dry land. "Yet as soon as the priests who carried the ark reached the Jordan and their feet touched the water's edge, the water from upstream stopped flowing...the priests who carried the ark of the covenant of the LORD stood firm on dry ground in the middle of the Jordan, while all Israel passed by until the whole nation had completed the crossing on dry ground" (Joshua 3:15-17).

This illustration challenges me. Am I the kind of leader who has to see the dry ground first? Or am I willing to get a little wet and a little dirty, to step into uncertainty and trust Him? How bold for God am I really?

Their Courage

The way they handled the giants in their lives was vastly different as well. When the Israelite spies explored the promised land and gave a report, Moses allowed the negative views of ten men to impact the opinions of the whole nation. God gave the assurance that He would go before them. The victory was certain. Caleb, one of the spies who held fast to God's promises, confirmed they should go by saying, "We should go up and take possession of the land, for we can certainly do it" (Numbers 13:30). But the people would not listen. The negativity grew and spread like wildfire throughout the camp. Moses was grieved when the people would not listen, but instead of standing strong, he threw himself down in front of them and pleaded. God was greatly displeased and thus started the 40-year period of wandering in the desert.

Joshua's courage and the Israelites' courage under his leadership were very different from that earlier generation's. Instead of focusing on fearing their enemy, they focused on purifying themselves, freeing their hearts from sin. Then they boldly went where God told them to go, did exactly as they were instructed, and conquered the promised land God's way.

Then Joshua went a step further. He wanted to put into perspective the fear that had kept the Israelites from the promised land for 40 years. So he made an example of their enemies' kings. Joshua 10:24 records a glorious moment for the children of Israel, "When they brought these kings to Joshua, he summoned all the men of Israel and said to the army commanders who had come with him, 'Come here and put your feet on the necks of these kings.' So, they came forward and placed their feet on their necks."

Henry and Richard Blackaby make this observation:

> The young Israelite soldiers had grown up in abject fear of these kings. They spent year after year squandering their youth in a barren desert while their aging parents feebly justified their disobedience to God by explaining that Canaan was populated with fierce, undefeatable giants. But now they'd seen these "giants" up close. Even their kings were ordinary men who could be humbled by God. Joshua wanted to remove any question from his soldiers' minds that when they walked obediently with God they were invincible. Throughout the remainder of Joshua's leadership there is no mention of his soldiers ever fearing their enemies.[10]

God gave the children of Israel victory and placed their fears under their feet. Joshua's quick, obedient heart inspired his followers to become quick, obedient people. In Moses' defense, Joshua had the advantage of learning from Moses' mistakes. Joshua saw Moses in his moments of complete obedience and God's blessing. He saw Moses in times of disobedience and God's punishment. He saw Moses die before getting to the promised land just as God said. Joshua saw Moses' great faith lived out, and despite Moses' mistakes, Joshua saw a hero. Joshua not only saw but he learned. He let what he saw have a profound effect on his life.

We have the same advantage that Joshua had. We have now seen these great heroes of faith who walked before us. We've observed, we've studied, we've pondered, we've learned. Now, what kind of difference will their lives have on the way we walk?

The story crescendos as God's people under Joshua's leadership take possession of the land. The long-awaited, promised land. The time has come for us to take possession of something as well. We must cross the river, shout the shouts, watch the walls tumble, and take possession of the promises of God.

Did you catch that theme in the background throughout this whole book? We've been in preparation to fully possess all the promises of God for ourselves. Webster's New World Dictionary defines *possess* as "(1) to have as belonging to one, to own; (2) to have as an attribute, quality; (3) to gain control over."

Isn't that a revealing definition? How applicable it is to our possession of the promises of God. We must first learn to take them as our own. Not that we own them exclusively but that we own them *personally.* We come to depend on God and His promises to instruct us, teach us, and lead us. Secondly, our possession of God's promises affects us. He shapes and molds our character. He redefines who we are and what we are about.

And lastly, God and His promises gain control over our lives. Our relationship with Him so profoundly changes us that we live completely different lives as a result. We truly become the new creation God intends for us to become. "Therefore, if anyone is in Christ, *he is a new creation;* the old has gone, the new has come!" (2 Corinthians 5:17). In order to possess God's promises in this way, we must surrender our old dependencies. <u>What else or who else rivals God for your dependence?</u>

Is it your parents? Your spouse? Your children? Your career? Your lifestyle? Your past accomplishments? <u>Whatever or whoever it is, let me encourage you to surrender these false props and depend on God alone to empower you.</u> Andy Stanley gives us this challenge:

> Your primary goal should be to live in an ongoing state of surrender, acknowledging that without the intervention of the Holy Spirit you will be defeated by the power of sin. If there is a singular theme that emerges from the entirety of Scripture, it is this: Through relationship with God, man is finally capable of doing that which he was incapable of doing on his own. That's what walking in the Spirit is all about. And that's what character is all about... Character is the by-product of dependency...Character is the will to do what is right, as defined by God, regardless of personal cost.[11]

Joshua was indeed a man of character. When the Israelites finally possessed the promised land and divided it among the tribes, Joshua was the last to receive his allotted portion. He made sure everyone got what they deserved before himself. He possessed his promised land, but even more importantly, he possessed God's promises.

I pray this is true for you as well. Walking with God takes you to amazing places, but even more importantly, it allows you to experience Him in amazing ways. We have not only experienced Him but hopefully we have also been transformed by Him. I feel it only appropriate to leave you with a part of Joshua's final speech to the people he loved so much. They had journeyed together. They had triumphed together. They had fallen deeply in love with God together. May it be so for us as well!

> You yourselves have seen everything the LORD your God has done to all these nations for your sake; it was the LORD who fought for you... Be very strong; be careful to obey all that is written in the Book of the Law of Moses, without turning aside to the right or to the left... You know with all your heart and soul that not one of these good promises the LORD your God gave you has failed. Every promise has been fulfilled; not one has failed (Joshua 23:3,6,14).

What happens when women walk in faith? Well, now you know my story.

Oh, sweet friend, what a privilege it has been to walk this part of your journey with you. My prayer is that you have a clearer vision of where you are in the phases of faith and that this knowledge will give you courage to press on. Though the adventure is harder and grander than we ever imagined, I hope you can now say without a doubt that walking with God does indeed take you to amazing places. Continue striving to become a woman who looks back on her walk with God with no regrets. For that, my friend, is the real dream.

Personal Bible Study

As we finish the book and Bible study, I would like to close with my prayer for you, my friend. Please look up these verses as I reference them, meditate on them, and make them your prayer for yourself as well. I pray that you would continually pray this prayer as you go forward in your walk with God.

I pray that when you hear His voice, you will not harden your hearts (Psalm 95:7-8; Hebrews 4:7-8).

I pray that you will live by faith and not by sight (2 Corinthians 5:7).

I pray that you will continue to grow in spiritual maturity (Colossians 4:12).

I pray that you will be able to understand the length, width, depth, and breadth of Christ's love for you (Ephesians 3:18-19).

I pray that you will always be eager to do the right thing (Hebrews 13:21).

I pray that the God of hope will fill you with much joy and peace while you trust in Him (Romans 15:13).

I pray that God would give you a spirit of wisdom and revelation (Ephesians 1:17).

I pray that you will be as loving as God and as patient as Christ (2 Thessalonians 3:5).

I pray that God will strengthen you with power through His Spirit (Ephesians 3:16).

I pray that you will get along with each other as well as Jesus got along with us all (Romans 15:5).

I pray that you will be on your face before the Lord, admitting your dependence on Him (James 4:10).

I pray that you will continue training for a godly life (1 Timothy 4:7).

And finally, I pray that you will continue to live in Christ, rooted and built up in Him, strengthened in the faith as you were taught and overflowing with thankfulness (Colossians 2:6).

Pray these prayers throughout your week and experience the power of praying God's Word. May your life be forever changed by your amazing walk with God. Amen and amen.

Notes

1. Joel Osteen, *Your Best Life Now* (New York: Warner Faith, 2004), 6.
2. Phillip Keller, *A Shepherd Looks at Psalm 23* (Grand Rapids, Michigan: Zondervan, 1970), 26-27.
3. Joyce Meyer, *In Pursuit of Peace* (New York: Warner Faith, 2004), 56.
4. *Life Application Study Bible,* New International Version (Wheaton, Illinois: Tyndale House Publishers, 1988), 269-97.
5. *Life Application Study Bible,* 127.
6. With thanks to Mark Hamby, whose sermon inspired these thoughts.
7. Max Lucado, *Come Thirsty* (Nashville: W Publishing Group, 2004), 121-22.
8. Quoted in Bob Buford, *Finishing Well* (Nashville: Integrity Publishers, 2004), 171.
9. Max Lucado, *When God Whispers Your Name* (Nashville: W Publishing Group, 1994), 165-66.
10. Henry Blackaby and Richard Blackaby, *Called to Be God's Leader: Lessons from the Life of Joshua* (Nashville: Thomas Nelson Publishers, 2004), 182-83.
11. Andy Stanley, *Louder than Words* (Sisters, Oregon: Multnomah, 2004), 35, 174-75.

About Lysa

Lysa TerKeurst is the president of Proverbs 31 Ministries and author of 21 books, including the *New York Times* bestsellers *Uninvited* and *The Best Yes*. Additionally, Lysa has been featured on *Focus on the Family*, *The Today Show*, *Good Morning America*, and more. Lysa speaks nationwide at Catalyst, Lifeway Abundance Conference, Women of Joy, and various church events.

She deeply loves her family and lives with them in Charlotte, North Carolina. Connect with Lysa on social media @LysaTerKeurst or on her blog at www.lysaterkeurst.com.

About Proverbs 31 Ministries

If you were inspired by *What Happens When Women Walk in Faith* and desire to deepen your own personal relationship with Jesus Christ, we have just what you're looking for.

Proverbs 31 Ministries exists to be a trusted friend who will take you by the hand and walk by your side, leading you one step closer to the heart of God through:

Free First 5 app

Free online daily devotions

Online Bible studies

Writer and speaker training

Daily radio programs

Books and resources

For more information about Proverbs 31 Ministries,
visit www.Proverbs31.org

More Lysa TerKeurst Books from Harvest House Publishers

What Happens When Women Say Yes to God

What Happens When Women Say Yes to God Devotional

What Happens When Women Say Yes to God DVD

What Happens When Women Say Yes to God Interactive Workbook

What Happens When Young Women Say Yes to God

Am I Messing Up My Kids?

Other Great Reads from Lysa TerKeurst

Finding I AM

Uninvited

The Best Yes

Becoming More Than a Good Bible Study Girl

Unglued

Made to Crave

Made to Crave for Young Women